ROCK GARDENS
& ALPINE PLANTS

DAVID JOYCE

TREASURE PRESS

Contents

Illustrations by

Kevin Maddison 33, 36, 37, 40, 41, 44, 45, 52, 53, 56, 57, 60, 61, 64, 65, 68, 69, 73, 76-77
David Salariya 8, 9, 25, 48, 49, 80, 81, 84, 85, 93
David Wright 4-5, 13, 21, 28-29

Acknowledgement
The following pictures were taken especially for Octopus Books:
Michael Boys 22-3, 30-1, 46, 51 above, 79, 83 below; Jerry Harpur 11, 18-9, 47, 66, 67, 70, 71, 75, 86, 90-1, 94; George Wright 7, 51 below, 58, 83 above 87.
The publishers also acknowledge the help of: Ardea 78; Biofotos 54, 59, Pat Bridley 39; George Hyde 55; David Joyce 63; Palma Studio 43; Harry Smith Horticultural Photographic Collection 74; Michael Warren 15.

First published in Great Britain in 1984 by
Octopus Books Limited

This edition published in 1987 by
Treasure Press
59 Grosvenor Street
London W1

ISBN 1 85051 176 4

Printed in Hong Kong

INTRODUCTION

For year-round interest, for versatility and for range of colour, texture and habit, rock plants stand out as an exceptional category of garden plants. Conditions in which they flourish and give a rewarding display are possible in almost any garden, no matter how small, and can be achieved with a modest outlay. Once established, rock plants are, for the greater part, long lived and remarkably free of pests and diseases.

Many rock plants are true alpines; dwarf herbaceous or sub-shrubby perennials adapted to harsh mountain conditions. In their natural habitats there is likely to be a fairly constant and abundant water supply but the soil is generally thin and gritty and drainage very sharp. If it were not for their hummocky and ground-hugging shapes and, in many cases, felted or hairy leaves, these plants would be shredded and desiccated by searing winds. In winter, sometimes for periods of several months, they are insulated from low temperatures and protected from surface wet by a blanket of snow.

When grown in garden conditions some alpines are highly temperamental, intolerant of dryness, slow drainage, freezing winter temperatures and, most of all, winter damp. They are

plants for the enthusiast, who will take pride in growing to perfection a range of delightful but demanding subjects.

In addition to the true alpines, there are many rock plants of dwarf and prostrate growth that are adapted to living in rugged and open terrain at lower altitudes. They include some of the easiest and most useful plants for creating broad and colourful effects.

Fortunately the days are past when rock gardens were rather literal miniaturizations of alpine landscapes, involving in their construction massive excavation and the moving of tonnes of heavy stone. Free-draining soil and an open position, the principal requirements of most rock plants, can be achieved with a minimum of labour and with relatively little rock. There are ways, too, of growing rock garden plants in which rock barely features. For example, there are numerous creeping and mat-forming plants that are happy growing in gaps left in paving of any kind. Raised beds, which can be of brick or stone, are perhaps the most versatile features for growing a wide range of rock plants. For the gardener with little space, concrete or stone sinks and troughs, even window boxes, can accommodate a remarkably large collection of interesting and beautiful plants.

For the purposes of this book the main dwarf herbaceous perennials and woody plants have been grouped together and separate sections have been devoted to bulbs, dwarf conifers and ferns and grasses, categories which are often neglected.

MAKING A ROCK GARDEN

PLANNING AND SITING Rock garden plants are of
such variety that some can be found to grow in almost any
aspect or under any conditions. However, most gardeners will
want to grow a fairly broad range of plants and with this in
mind it is worth taking some trouble to plan and site a garden.
Building entails some heavy labour so it is important to get it
right the first time round.

There are three basic requirements that need to be satisfied if
a rock garden is to be successful. There must be adequate
drainage. Although a large number of alpines and other rock
plants need a plentiful supply of water, the water must never be
stagnant. A suitable site must, therefore, be one where, if
drainage is not already good, it can be improved artificially.

The position should be sheltered from cutting winds. In the
larger garden it may be possible to provide a certain degree of
shelter by planting shrubs at the edge of a rock garden. The
problem is often more acute in the small garden, where walls
and fences can channel fiercely turbulent cold air.

A third requirement is that the position should be relatively
open and free from overhanging branches. Dripping from
overhead foliage is a more serious problem than light shade.

An ideal position is a gentle south-facing slope linking two
levels in the garden. However, a natural slope is by no means
essential and rock can be used on a level site to build up
terraces with a predominantly south-facing aspect.

Cost may prove a major factor limiting the amount of rock
you are able to use. One of your first steps should be to visit a
quarry or nursery where you can buy suitable rock. Try to use a
local stone if possible, it will be more in keeping with the
surroundings. If you have not already had experience of
building a rock garden it is difficult to visualize the amount of
rock needed for a given site. The advice of a reliable firm will
be of great value.

A large part of the cost will be incurred in transporting the
rock so look for a supply close by. When building a
natural-looking feature, resist the temptation to supplement
rock with man-made materials, even if you have, for instance, a
ready supply of old bricks. If you cannot afford as much rock
as you need, consider constructing a raised bed. In a more
formal feature of this kind, man-made materials do not look
out of place.

Two other considerations should be borne in mind. You
should consider how the rock garden will appear from various
angles, particularly from the house. Finally, you should take
into account ease of access during construction.

PROVIDING CONDITIONS FOR GROWTH A first
and vital step in preparing the site for a rock garden is
thorough weeding and in particular the eradication of all
perennial weeds. It is difficult to overstate the importance of
this preparatory stage; perennial weeds that are not eradicated
will become established in rockwork and you may have to use
remedies that will be harmful to cultivated plants. Badly
infested ground that is being prepared for a rock garden may
require treatment with a chemical weedkiller; in the case of
persistent kinds, this could delay construction for several
months.

The second major step is to ensure that drainage is adequate.
On a raised or sloping site it is unlikely that bottom drainage
will be a problem. However, where there is doubt about free
drainage, it is worth excavating to a depth of 15-30cm (6-12in)
and filling with a mixture of stones and broken brick covered
with a layer of gravel. Adequate drainage is vital for all rock
garden plants, though some, such as *Fritillaria meleagris*,
prefer damp conditions.

The acid/alkaline character of a soil and rock can have a
marked effect on the plants you can grow. The pH scale is the
standard measure of acid/alkaline content in a soil. On this
scale the neutral point is 7; readings below this point indicate
an increase in acidity and readings above it an increase in
alkalinity. You are already likely to know whether your soil is
markedly alkaline or markedly acid. If you do not, it is worth

Cassiope lycopodioides

testing before you begin to build a rock garden.

When choosing rock, it is worth considering the materials that are most versatile. The sandstones are useful because all plants will grow in association with them particularly the lime-hating plants such as cassiope and the ericas. When first quarried they are soft but develop a hard skin when they are exposed to weather. It is generally possible to detect the stratification, which should always run horizontally when the rocks are bedded. If rocks are placed so that the stratification runs vertically, they may be split and shattered by frost action.

Limestone is often attractively worn and fretted and has long been popular as a material for gardens where lime-tolerant plants are to be grown. Some forms are even so hard that under normal conditions the lime in the stone is not readily soluble and even lime-haters can be grown in association with them.

Most rock garden plants do not require a rich soil and if given one grow with an unnatural luxuriance that makes them vulnerable to winter damage. The basic mixture, which will satisfy most plants, should consist of one part of medium loam, one part of humus (which can be leaf mould or moss peat) and two parts of gritty sand or rock chippings. To this can be added a light dusting of a slow-acting fertilizer such as bone meal.

As a finishing touch, the rock garden will need a layer of rock chippings about 2.5cm (1in) deep. Only use limestone chippings here and in the soil mixture if lime-tolerant plants are to be grown. The chippings will act as a mulch.

Fritillaria meleagris

WATER IN THE ROCK GARDEN

In almost any garden the introduction of water, even on a small scale, adds an attractive dimension. In the rock garden a well-placed pool or a sequence of pools with running water can heighten the effect of a wild natural landscape created by the rocks and plants. The addition of water also provides an opportunity to grow numerous plants that complement alpines and rock plants.

Re-working an established rock garden to accommodate a water feature may involve the moving of heavy rock and the lifting of established plants. It is therefore ideal to plan water features as an integral part of the rock garden right from the beginning. A later addition is so often fitted in where it is likely to cause the least work and this may not be the most visually satisfying solution.

A pool should have two levels; the main body, about 75cm (30in) deep, and a margin, about 25cm (10in) deep. It is best situated where it will be in full sun for at least half the day.

Construction in concrete is laborious and requires experience to get a really satisfactory result. A leaking pool is worse than no pool at all. Prefabricated fibreglass pools are strong and easy to install although they are somewhat expensive. It is necessary to excavate a hole slightly larger than the pool itself and then to use sand or fine soil as a backing layer to give the pool support. The lip needs to be concealed with an edging of rock to make it look as natural as possible.

The least expensive and one of the most satisfactory methods of construction is to use a pool liner, made out of PVC, for example, laid on a bed of sand spread on the base of the hole. The sand must be free of sharp stones otherwise there is a danger that the liner might be punctured. The rim of such a pool will also need to be disguised by an edging of rock.

If a series of pools are to be connected by running water some form of pumping system will be needed to circulate the water. The installation of electrical equipment, such as a submerged water pump, should be carried out by a qualified electrician. However, these pumps do tend to clog up and so it is important to keep your pool water as clean as possible. The best way to do this is to install oxygenating plants.

A pool liner can also be used to form a small bog garden, the ideal companion to the rock pool. The liner should be laid in a hole about 30cm (12in) deep with drainage holes cut in about 15cm (6in) from the bottom. The bed can be filled with a loamy compost over turves that have been laid grass-side down.

If a pool is to be a feature that really enhances the rock garden, its planting should be on a scale with the rest. The pool itself can be planted with deep-water and marginal water plants. What will give it a really authentic touch are the bog plants surrounding it. These could include some of the moisture-loving astilbes, primulas and ferns, as well as many other beautiful plants. Oxygenating plants include water moss (*Fontinalis antipyretica*).

CONSTRUCTING THE ROCK GARDEN The
construction of a rock garden involves moving very heavy
items. Even if you are reasonably fit, the work should be taken
slowly and carefully; injuries can happen, particularly if your
experience is limited. You should make sure that you have the
proper equipment and you should be able to call on the help of
other people when it is necessary. One or two sturdy but
patient assistants is the ideal.

It is likely that you will not have all the tools you need as part
of your normal garden equipment. Rather than improvize, hire
equipment such as crowbars, rollers and a sack truck. Planking
will be necessary for trucking rock across lawns and soft
ground. Try to be available when the rock is delivered so that
you can make sure it is dropped in a position that is convenient
for the work of construction.

Once you have decided on the possible site in your garden,
mark it out with pegs and string to a slightly larger size than
you envisage for the final effect. Try to imagine the height of
the garden; this is more difficult but is vital if the rock garden is
to look in proportion to the rest of your garden — you don't
want a mountain or a molehill.

On a gently sloping site (above right), the aim should be to
convey the impression of irregular terraced outcrops. For each
terrace, select a large rock, a keystone, which should be
positioned more or less centrally. Smaller rocks can then be
placed on either side to form the arms of an L-shape or two
gently curving arcs. Don't use rocks that are too small; the
garden will be more stable with sturdy, larger stones. The
further they are from the keystone, the shallower they will be in
the soil. Start from the base, bedding the rocks firmly about
7.5-15cm (3-6in) deep. A slight backward tilt will increase the
impression that these are rocky outcrops and lead water back
into the pocket behind. As each tier is built up the soil mixture
should be filled in behind.

On a flat site (below right), the method of construction is
basically the same but the height has to be achieved by tiers of
rocky outcrops holding in the soil. Start by bedding in a large
keystone and work out from it with companion rocks to form
the first terrace. Although occasional random stones may be
used between tiers, the essential structure should be ordered so
that pockets of soil are created between apparently natural
outcrops. The natural effect can be enhanced by having the
slope on some sides much steeper than on others; planting
with trailing rock plants can take advantage of these cliff-like
faces. It is well worth casting a critical eye over other rock
gardens, particularly those in botanic gardens, to see how
natural effects have been achieved and what pitfalls need to be
avoided. You can also note which plants are used in which
positions in the garden. A botanic garden is an ideal place to sit
and plan your garden on paper.

Some planting can be done as construction is carried out,

especially where you want to lodge a plant in a crevice. The main planting should be left for several weeks at least, for there will be some settlement of the soil. Retain some spare mixture for topping up. The layer of rock chippings can be added once the main planting has been done.

Cross-section of a rock garden on a sloping site.

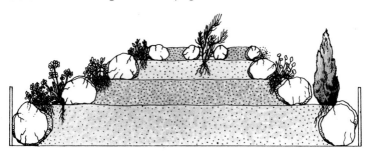

Planning a rock garden on a flat site.

Keystone

RAISED BEDS FOR EASY CULTIVATION In the

small garden there are few more satisfactory ways of growing
an attractive range of rock plants than in a raised bed, which
can be made from a wide variety of materials. In some
situations there is little chance of making a natural-looking
rock garden and in such circumstances a more formal raised
bed is a much better solution.

Once they have been built, raised beds are well suited to
being tended by the elderly or the physically disabled. Provided
a bed is built to an appropriate height and width and access is
satisfactory, preferably on firm paving, a gardener can do
planting and general maintenance from a wheelchair.

The many materials that can be used for building raised beds
include natural and artificial rock, masonry, brick, concrete
and wood in the form of railway sleepers. A raised bed may
even be a useful way of using materials, such as brick and
masonry, from a demolished building.

When selecting the site and preparing for planting, similar
considerations as apply in siting a rock garden must be taken
into account. The ground on which the bed is to be built
should be free of perennial weeds and a base of rubble topped
with gravel provided to allow for free drainage. Raised beds
can be used to grow plants above ground that is naturally
poorly drained. In such cases additional rubble will need to be
put in to form a bottom layer about 30cm (12in) deep.

Beds can be built in a variety of shapes to fit in to the area
available but simple oblongs, circles, arcs and L-shapes are the
most convenient. If the raised bed is for a disabled gardener, it
should be relatively narrow so that the centre can be reached
without too much trouble. The method of construction will
depend on the materials being used but the first requirements
must be stability of the walls and adequate allowance for
drainage at the base, if, for instance, concrete or mortar is used.
If a drystone wall is being built, fill in with the soil mixture as
construction proceeds. The same mixture of two parts grit to
one part loam and one part humus as is used in the rock
garden is appropriate here. It can be an opportunity, if your soil
is naturally chalky, to make beds that are lime-free. If this is
your intention, you will need to buy in lime-free loam. Fill the
bed nearly to the top with the soil mixture and leave for several
weeks to allow for settlement.

In a broad raised bed it is useful to have one or two large
stepping stones and even where the bed is narrow it is
desirable to have a few reasonably sized rocks breaking
through the surface. Many plants will benefit from the cool
root-run they provide.

A raised bed can be planted in much the same way and with
the same range of plants as a rock garden but particular
attention should be given to planting trailing subjects that will
break the rather formal edge. Use a layer of rock chippings as a
mulch to suppress weeds and retain moisture.

MAKING A SCREE GARDEN

A striking feature of alpine landscapes is the sloping beds of broken rock which are constantly fed with new material that has been produced by wind, rain and forest action weathering the substance of mountains. In these endlessly shifting bodies, rock plants sometimes lodge themselves and in the more stable moraines that have been left by glacial action, some of the greatest treasures of the alpine flora can be found. A modest version of the scree or moraine can be tailored to the garden.

An ideal position to site a scree garden is a gentle slope facing south. The plants that do well in these conditions are lovers of open sunny positions so there should be no shade cast by nearby trees or shrubs. The scree garden can work quite satisfactorily as an isolated feature but is most successful when it forms an integral part of a large rock garden.

As with any kind of rock garden, a first step must be to ensure the eradication of all perennial weeds. Provided a suitable slope exists, the scree garden is easy to construct. The essential requirement is good drainage, which can be assured by laying drainage tiles at the bottom of the slope.

Excavate the slope to a depth of approximately 50cm (20in) and then fork over and loosen the base. Replace the excavated soil to about half its depth with a fairly gritty mixture — about three parts of chippings to one part of loam and one part of

A scree garden construction with a slope of between 1 in 10 and 1 in 20 — the 25cm (10in) layer of soil is topped with 25cm (10in) of gravel.

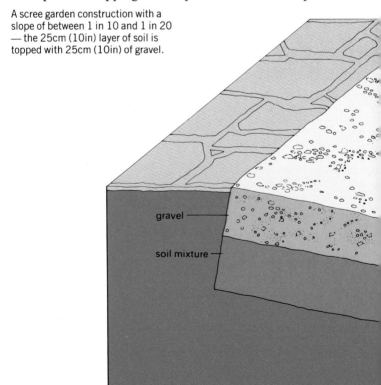

gravel

soil mixture

moss peat. This mixture should be topped with a layer of about the same thickness of rock chippings. An alternative is to have a thicker layer of an even coarser mixture topped by about 5cm (2in) of chippings. The addition of a few large rocks will provide useful stepping stones and break up a surface that might otherwise look monotonously flat. The occasional large rock will also give cool root conditions.

When planting up a scree garden, you are in effect putting pot-grown plants with soil around their root ball into 25cm (10in) of stones. The stones will support the plant until its roots have grown in search of the moisture and food below. In a normal garden, plants tend to send their roots in all directions. If you water scree garden plants and the drainage is such that water flows downwards, the lower foliage will not rot.

Some vigorous plants will grow quite happily in the scree but it is better to use this kind of garden for the cushion- and rosette-forming miniatures. These could include armerias, campanulas, dianthus, lewisias, raoulias and saxifrages.

Where the soil is chalky it is better not to struggle against nature and to confine planting to lime-tolerant plants. On a neutral or acid soil it is possible to include lime for the real lime-lovers but this should only be done at the base of the scree so that there is no chance of lime seeping to parts where lime-haters might be grown.

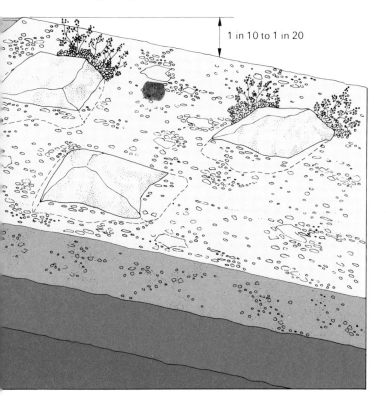

1 in 10 to 1 in 20

MINIATURE ROCK GARDENS

The dwarf, even miniature, character of so many rock garden plants makes them really useful subjects for small scale gardening. There may be no room for any of the features in which rock garden plants are generally grown but the smallest paved yard can accommodate one or more sinks or troughs containing a delightful mixture of tiny plants. There is even scope for this kind of garden on a balcony or with plants grown in window boxes.

The most attractive and sought-after containers for growing rock plants are old stone sinks and troughs. They are now, unfortunately, difficult to come by and expensive but there is a rightness about them that other containers cannot quite match. The most suitable substitutes are old-fashioned glazed sinks, which can be coated with a rough mixture of peat, sand and cement so that they have a natural weathered appearance. Although they are not expensive, they are increasingly difficult to find. Among other possibilities are containers made of concrete or fibreglass and containers constructed from old railway sleepers. Weight may be an important consideration for balconies and window boxes but, all other considerations taken into account, when it is not possible to use stone, the container should be as inconspicuous as possible so that the

plants, not the container, become the focus of attention.

Once a container has been filled and planted, it will be very difficult to move, almost impossible if it is a stone sink. It is, therefore, worth planning its position with great care. You will need to consider light and shade if there are particular categories of plants you want to grow and access must also be taken into account. Sink gardens raised to a convenient height are attractive features for the disabled gardener. Bear in mind, for instance, access by wheelchair. When a position has been decided upon, raise the container on supports so that water can get away through drainage holes without difficulty. If necessary, adjust the height of the supports to make the best display or to allow easy working.

The mixture used to fill the container will depend on the kind of plants you want to grow, particularly on whether they are lime-lovers or lime-haters. A good general mixture consists of two parts potting compost, such as John Innes No. 1, and one part coarse sand. Fill the container to within 5cm (2in) of the top and bed in one or two pieces of rock to suggest an outcrop. Allow the mixture to settle before planting and top up with a layer of chippings. Plant sparingly, exploiting differences of texture and habit to give these miniature gardens year-round interest.

PLANTS IN PAVING AND TUFA STONE
Many rock plants can be grown quite satisfactorily in a flat garden among paving. Used in this way they can do much to soften what might otherwise be a rather stark area and they can even successfully disguise harsh and unattractive paving. Some plants will tolerate a certain amount of treading but planting should not intrude on the main lines of access.

Where there is sufficient soil beneath existing paving and there are adequate gaps between slabs, say 2.5cm (1in), it will be possible to introduce plants quite successfully. Most of the plants that are suitable require open sunny positions and this should be borne in mind when planting. The most appropriate time to plant is in early autumn when there is a good chance that roots will be able to take hold without the plant having to fight drought. Small young plants have the greatest chance of getting established. Excavate as much as possible of the sub-soil, using a sharp knife or an old kitchen fork, and replace with a basic rock garden mixture. Set the plant as deeply as possible but with rock chippings worked around the neck.

Several easy plants can be established most satisfactorily by sowing seed. This should be done in spring, care being taken that weeds do not get a hold and swamp the seedlings.

If you are laying new paving it is possible to ensure reasonable growing conditions for plants and adequate gaps for them to grow in. Paving is generally laid over a bed of sand, which is itself laid over rubble. If you plan to grow rock plants to make the most of your paving, it is worth introducing a layer of basic rock garden compost over the rubble. Provided it is well stamped down, slabs of paving can be laid directly on this; alternatively, a reduced layer of sand can be used. Avoid a random arrangement of gaps.

The selection of plants will depend to some extent on whether the underlying soil is limy or acidic. Some of the small bulbs, particularly crocuses, and grasses can be used effectively. Among sub-shrubby and herbaceous plants some of the best include armerias, dianthus, ericas, geraniums, phloxes, saxifrages, sedums and sempervivums.

Tufa stone is a curious natural material that has the appearance of petrified grey froth. It is exceptionally light but is expensive and often difficult to obtain. Despite the fact that it contains lime, most plants will grow in association with it quite happily. It is an easy matter to bore a hole in it either with a drill or a hammer and chisel and miniature alpines that are inserted and plugged in will take root and thrive. To ensure that the plants will be secure and will not dry out, plug two thirds of the hole with a little mortar (five parts of sand to one part of cement).

Tufa can be used as the basic stone in a small rock garden, as outcrops in a scree or raised bed and it is especially effective as part of a trough or sink garden. A large piece can even be used in isolation to grow cushion- and rosette-forming plants.

A PEAT BED

Most of the plants popularly considered appropriate to the rock garden are those that do well in sunny open situations. There are, however, many dwarf plants, mainly woodlanders, that thrive in light shade and are, therefore, useful in some parts of the rock garden or raised bed, particularly in north-facing positions. There are, in addition, numerous plants, including practically the whole of the vast genus *Rhododendron*, that are markedly intolerant of lime. Lime-haters and shade-lovers can be brought together attractively in a special kind of raised bed made from peat blocks.

A peat bed can be built on soil of any kind, including that containing lime. In fact, where the main soil is alkaline a peat bed offers by far the most satisfactory way of growing these plants that are intolerant of lime. Avoid a hot south-facing position, where full exposure to sun will dry out blocks too quickly, and positions directly under trees, where leaf drip can be a problem. An ideal site is a slightly sloping north-facing position or one where there is dappled shade provided by shrubs or trees growing at some distance.

Peat blocks, which are available from specialist nurseries and garden centres, should be approximately $30 \times 10 \times 10$cm ($12 \times 4 \times 4$in) and larger if possible. Smaller blocks dry out too quickly. Those described as 'top spit' are longest lasting for they contain roots that hold the peat together. A mixture of

Rhododendron obtusum

peat or leaf mould and lime-free loam can be used for the bed.
The constituents should be thoroughly mixed — a little
slow-release general fertilizer can be added in the process,
before being forked into the bed.

The shape of the bed will depend very much on the space
available. In general, the simpler the bed, the more stable it will
be. In any case thoughtful selection and positioning of plants
will break up any rigidity that may be apparent in the bare bed
at first.

Before building, soak the blocks thoroughly by immersing
them in water for at least one day. The lowest course of the
blocks, which are laid flat, should be bedded slightly below
surface level in order to give stability. Lay the blocks in the
same way as you would lay bricks, so that the vertical joints are
overlapped by a brick in the next layer. Fill in the bed as
construction advances, making it really firm. Walls should not
go much higher than 50cm (20in); they can be given additional
stability by driving spikes through them at intervals of about
1m (40in).

The walls can be planted during construction but as plants
are so easily worked in there is little advantage in doing this.
The root systems of plants inserted in the walls will help to
bind the blocks together. Before planting the bed, allow it to
settle for a week or so. Thorough drenching of the bed will help
it to settle.

STOCKING THE ROCK GARDEN

OBTAINING PLANTS   There is no shortage of choice in
building up a collection of rock garden plants. It is tempting in
an initial planting to leave very little bare ground but allowance
should be made for the spreading habit of so many suitable
plants. Selection will depend on personal taste but it is worth
trying to strike a balance between easy-going and free-
flowering plants that are often vigorous spreaders and the
quieter plants of refined and subtle beauty. It is generally not
advisable to plant these two groups in close proximity but in
most gardens there will be space for both.

   The richness and complexity of the vegetable world is such
that common names are inadequate as a way of referring to the
many highly desirable rock garden plants. In this book the
scientific method of naming as used in garden catalogues and
at nurseries and garden centres has been used. In this system a
plant name has two main parts. For instance, the scientific
name of the maiden pink is *Dianthus deltoides*. *Dianthus* is
the name of the genus, the classification of plants to which all
pinks belong, and *deltoides* added to it indicates the particular
species, the group of plants in the genus *Dianthus* that in all
important respects are the same.

   Some species show certain variations, for instance of size, in
the wild and in cultivation and these variations have been
greatly exploited horticulturally. Additional names are added
to distinguish them; those that arise in cultivation are given a
cultivar name, which is printed in roman type (genus and
species names are printed in italics) and enclosed in single
quotes.

   Nurseries and garden centres offer the herbaceous and
sub-shrubby perennials as pot-grown plants, nurseries
despatching mail orders in spring and autumn. In fact, because
plants are pot grown, they can be put into the ground at almost
any time of the year, provided attention is paid to watering in
dry weather. The range of plants available in garden centres
tends to be rather limited and whimsically chosen. If you are
seriously interested in rock garden plants it is worth getting the
catalogues of some of the specialist nurseries, often modest
establishments but they do offer remarkable lists at good value.

   Try to see plants at different times of the year. It is generally
believed that spring is the best time to view plants in nurseries,
when so many of the alpines are in flower. However, if you
want colour and interest throughout the year, it is better to see
what plants look like at other times too.

   No matter how prodigal Nature seems to be, resist the
temptation wherever you are to take plant material of whatever

kind in the wild. You may save yourself a brush with the law in the country you are visiting and any country into which you subsequently import plant material. You will probably be spared a disappointing failure (for transplanting from the wild requires special skills) and, most importantly, you will have done nothing to damage a threatened heritage. Indiscriminate collecting has been a major factor in reducing populations of plants to perilously low levels that until relatively recently may have been not at all uncommon. The mobility of the modern tourist may contribute further to the dangers that wild plant populations face.

Close observation of plants in the wild is, however, one of the greatest pleasures the rock gardener can enjoy, providing inspiration for the wild landscape at home.

To increase your stock of Pulsatilla, the seed heads should be teased out and flattened on the surface of the sowing compost.

PROPAGATION

Most gardeners will begin their collection of rock garden plants by buying them or by being given growing plants. To increase that collection by propagating your own plants — including plants that you can use as swap material with other gardeners — is not complicated and is a satisfying part of rock gardening.

Division, a simple method of vegetative propagation, is suitable for plants with fibrous roots; it is best carried out between autumn and spring. Old perennials often become woody and bare at the centre so periodic division is a good way of rejuvenating your stock. Clump-forming plants often become a tangle of growth and every two or three years they will need splitting up. Do this carefully by discarding the older inner part of the clump and replanting the new outer growth. This can be done while the plant is in the ground (1) with two small forks back to back or you can lift the plant that is to be divided and separate off sections from the periphery, each section with a good root system.

A high proportion of rock garden plants can be propagated by taking cuttings, which is particularly suitable for the forms of plants that do not come true from seed. The material for cuttings should be non-flowering shoots on healthy plants. The best time for taking cuttings is in most instances after flowering in mid-summer, although soft cuttings of many plants can also be taken in spring or early summer. Cuttings of conifers need to be taken in the autumn. Take small stems, about 5cm (2in) long (2), in the case of semi-hardwood cuttings with a heel of older wood (3), trim off the lower leaves and insert up to the

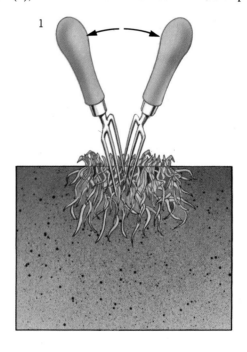

1

remaining leaves in pots containing a damp mixture of equal parts of coarse sand and peat. Dipping the cuttings in a combined hormone-rooting powder and fungicide before inserting them in the compost will encourage early rooting. Place the cuttings in a shaded position, preferably in a close frame to maintain high humidity, and ensure that the compost is kept moist. Any cuttings that show signs of mould should be discarded immediately. When the cuttings have rooted they should be potted up individually in a richer compost and grown on before being planted out. This is best done in peat pots. You will then not need to disturb the plant's root system when you plant out.

Unlike many bedding and border ornamentals, the plants grown in rock gardens include many species that will come true from seed. Nonetheless, there is always the chance in the open garden of hybridization occurring between species of the same genus, particularly so in some genera, such as *Aquilegia* and *Lewisia*. Although the seed of only a small range of rock garden plants is available commercially, specialist societies arrange distributions of seeds and from these it is possible to build up stocks of often quite uncommon and interesting plants.

It is not always easy to know when is the best time to sow rock garden plants. Some only germinate freely when the seed is sown freshly ripe; some require a period of intense cold for the germination process to be triggered off. As a general rule sow seed as soon as it becomes available and, if you have sufficient of it, make a second sowing in the spring.

2

3

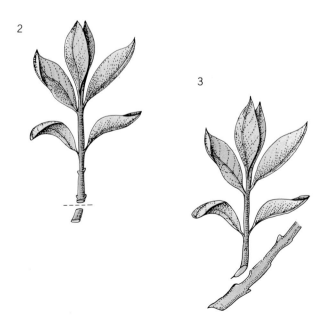

Use clean 7cm (3in) pots, preferably clay ones, or a seed tray and a rather gritty seed compost, such as the John Innes seed-sowing compost to which a small amount of sand has been added (4). Before sowing, wet the compost thoroughly by standing the pot in a basin of water or with a rose attachment on the watering can. Sow small seed directly on the surface; very fine seed is best first mixed with a little silver sand. Large seed should be covered to its own depth. Even distribution of seed, whatever the size, is very important and sowing too thickly is one of the commonest causes of poor results. A thin layer of fine chippings will discourage weeds and moss. Keep pots watered in a shady open frame facing north until germination. Alpine seeds do not need heat during germination, and except during wet weather, no frame cover. To reduce the need for watering, plunge the pots into coarse sand or grit. During rain, a glass or plastic cover at an angle will

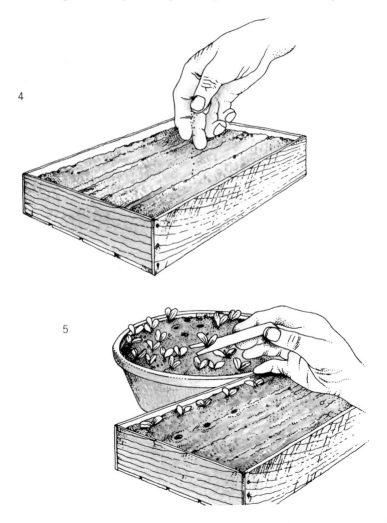

4

5

reduce drips from condensation. Seedlings can be transplanted once the first true leaves have developed (5). As some alpines may take more than a year to germinate, pots of seeds should be kept for at least two years after sowing.

Layering is a simple method of propagation, particularly for plants with woody stems at ground level, such as rhododendrons. Choose flexible branches and make a small cut in the lower side of the branch where it touches the ground. Bury it in the soil, holding it down with a pin and a stone if necessary (6), to a depth of 2cm (¾in). The new plant should have rooted by the following spring and it can then be cut free from its parent and transplanted.

Less common techniques that are useful with some plants include propagation from root cuttings, from leaf cuttings, from rooted suckers and, in the case of bulbous plants, from bulbils.

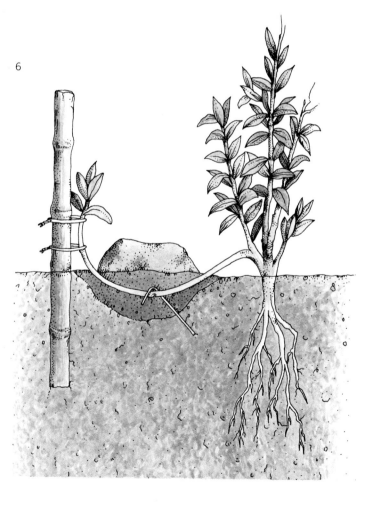

6

DEALING WITH PESTS

Provided that in other respects they are healthy, rock garden plants are to a remarkable degree less vulnerable to pests than many other ornamentals. There are, however, common pests that will attack and on plants of diminutive size the effects can be devastating in a short time.

Although many tough-leaved and robust rock garden plants are rarely attacked, slugs and snails have a cruel knack of destroying choice and favoured plants just as they are promising to fulfil the dreams you have had for them. They are pests that can be particularly dangerous in mild damp weather in early spring but they can strike a fatal blow — in the open garden or in a frame containing seedlings — at almost any time of the year. Proprietary slug baits offer the most convenient method of control and should be used as a precaution in the vicinity of particularly vulnerable plants before attacks occur. Take care when using these if you have pets or children who may play nearby.

Aphids tend to be more a problem for the specialist growing alpines under glass than for the gardener growing plants in the open. However, they have such a phenomenal capacity to multiply, building up colonies that sap the strength of plants, that prompt steps should be taken to control infestations. The fact that they are potential carriers of harmful viruses is

Crocus chrysanthus 'E. A. Bowles' (left) and *C.c.* 'Warley'

another powerful reason for taking action swiftly. There are a number of systemic insecticides available that, once absorbed by the plant, make it toxic to such pests for a period of a few weeks.

In spring particularly, birds are the most conspicuous nuisance in the rock garden and can do considerable damage. They will often vandalize early bulbs as they come into flower (yellow crocuses seem especially vulnerable) and attack small cushion-forming plants with brutal ferocity, tearing them to shreds. There is, unfortunately, no remedy that is aesthetically agreeable. The most reliable and least offensive precaution is to string up a criss-cross web of black cotton on twigs so that it just clears vulnerable plants. Although even this arrangement is somewhat unsightly, it is worth tolerating for the safety of plants, especially in early spring.

Mice can be the cause of considerable damage to bulbs and corms in the ground or in storage. Bulbs in store can be netted and mice populations controlled by trapping but outdoors there is no really effective control.

Of other pests that may from time to time cause problems, caterpillars are best dealt with by hand-picking while cutworms in the soil can be checked by applications of BHC powder.

WEED AND DISEASE CONTROL
In the established rock garden the most tiresome chore is probably that of weeding. Nonetheless, it is a job that must be taken seriously for weeds pose a really serious threat to dwarf plants, crowding them for space and competing with them for nutrients and water.

It has already been made clear that the eradication of perennial weeds must be a first step in preparing a site for a rock garden. They may be plants, like dandelion and dock, with thick and deep-reaching roots; bulbs, such as some species of *Allium* or *Oxalis*, that produce vast numbers of bulbils; or members of a large group of pernicious weeds — including bindweed, clover, couch grass and ground elder — that extend their territory by means of runners or stolons. Spending time to ensure eradication in the initial stages will save subsequent hours of difficult labour.

Even when great care has been taken in the preparatory stages, there is still the danger of perennial weeds germinating from seed or being introduced by other means. One of the commonest ways these plants are introduced is as seed or as very young plants with new stock brought into the garden. All bought stock, and for that matter whatever comes by way of a

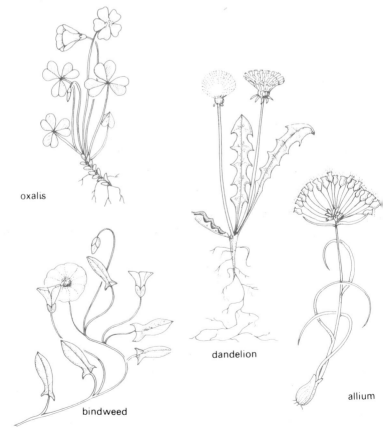

oxalis

dandelion

allium

bindweed

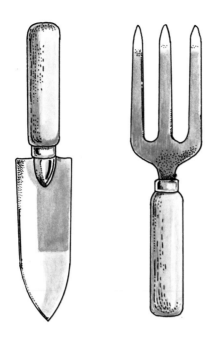

gift from other gardeners, should be closely examined for any sign of weeds growing with the new plant. By keeping alert, it should be possible to remove all perennial weeds at the first sign, even if this may mean risking the sacrifice of a plant with which the weed is entangled. Failure may mean perennial weeds gaining a hold. They will spread their roots under stones and in crevices; once they are established there may be no alternative to dismantling rockwork to get rid of them. Some of the new weedkillers that can be applied to the leaves of weeds offer the hope of a radical improvement in control.

Even when sterilized soil has been used in the construction of a rock garden and there is a weed-inhibiting mulch of chippings, annual weeds will eventually appear. Among the most troublesome are annual grass, chickweed, club moss, groundsel and shepherd's purse. Annual grass is a particular nuisance, with a talent for lodging itself in the heart of choice plants. The earlier weed seedlings are dealt with the better; a major battle has been lost when weeds are mature enough to flower and seed. Working over the rock garden with a hoe at any opportunity will kill weeds before they have a chance to become robust. Selective weedkillers can only be used with great caution so that if annual weeds are allowed to get away there may be hours of handweeding ahead of you.

It would be misleading to give the impression that rock garden plants are completely free of diseases but on the whole it is true that they are little troubled. When plants are attacked by viruses and fungi, ruthless elimination is probably the soundest course.

PLANTING FOR MAXIMUM EFFECT

Although there is a remorselessness about the pattern of the seasons, they do not necessarily fit into a neat division of months. Latitude and altitude are among the factors that will affect their timing and duration. Even in the same locality there can be variations of several weeks from year to year in the perceived arrival of spring to the onset of winter. Flowering times of particular plants reflect these annual variations. The listing below of plants by genus is intended to give an indication season by season of the flowering riches of the rock garden.

EARLY SPRING

Alyssum
Androsace
Chionodoxa
Crocus
Daphne
Erythronium
Galanthus
Iris
Muscari
Narcissus
Primula
Saxifraga
Sanguinaria
Scilla
Tulipa

MID-SPRING

Alyssum
Androsace
Arabis
Aubrieta
Cheiranthus
Cytisus
Dicentra
Erythronium
Gentiana
Hepatica
Leucojum
Muscari
Narcissus
Primula
Pulsatilla
Ramonda
Rhododendron
Saxifraga
Tulipa

LATE SPRING

Aethionema
Achillea
Aquilegia
Armeria
Aubrieta
Campanula
Cheiranthus
Cytisus
Dicentra
Dryas
Genista
Gentiana
Geum
Gypsophila
Iberis
Phlox
Phyteuma
Potentilla
Pulsatilla
Rhododendron
Saponaria
Scilla
Tulipa
Veronica
Viola

EARLY SUMMER

Achillea
Alchemilla
Allium
Androsace
Aquilegia
Aster
Aubrieta
Dianthus

Dicentra
Genista
Geranium
Geum
Helianthemum
Gypsophila
Hebe
Hypericum
Iberis
Leontopodium
Papaver
Phlox
Sedum
Rhododendron
Veronica
Viola

MID-SUMMER

Alyssum
Astilbe
Cyclamen
Dianthus
Campanula
Gentiana
Geranium
Hebe
Helianthemum
Hypericum
Phlox
Penstemon
Potentilla
Sedum
Sempervivum
Viola

LATE SUMMER

Alyssum
Calluna
Cyclamen
Gentiana
Oenothera
Papaver
Potentilla
Viola

EARLY AUTUMN
Calluna
Crocus

Cyclamen
Gentiana

MID-AUTUMN

Calluna
Cyclamen
Gentiana

LATE AUTUMN

Cyclamen
Erica
Galanthus
Gentiana

EARLY WINTER

Cyclamen
Erica

MID-WINTER

Crocus
Cyclamen
Erica
Galanthus
Iris
Saxifraga

LATE WINTER

Aubrieta
Chionodoxa
Crocus
Daphne
Erythronium
Galanthus
Iris
Muscari
Narcissus
Primula
Saxifraga
Scilla

GENERAL CARE General maintenance of the rock garden is not arduous, although it may require some agility and quite a lot of bending, and gives a welcome opportunity to inspect closely the miniature charm of many plants.

In the summer months especially — although short periods of drought may also occur at other times of the year — watering may be necessary. In the case of most alpines, the love of gritty free-draining soil goes with a need for a plentiful supply of sweet moving water. Although some rock plants show a remarkable capacity to revive after drought, there are many for whom neglect will be fatal. When watering is necessary it should be done really thoroughly. Heavy watering every two or three days during drought is much more beneficial than more frequent light sprinklings. If weather is very hot shortly after planting it is worth placing an object, such as a rock or a plank of wood standing upright, so as to cast shadow over young plants.

Several of the vigorous spreading rock plants, including alyssums and aubrietas, benefit from being clipped over with shears after flowering. They tend to become bare and loose over a period of two to three years if neglected but will remain compact as a result of trimming and may even produce a second smaller crop of flowers later in the season. In autumn check the growth of spreaders that threaten smaller plants.

On the established garden give plants a top dressing in spring or autumn. Scrape back the chippings and remove the

Raoulia australis

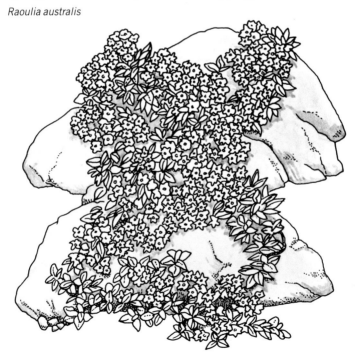

top layer of old soil, replacing with the standard mixture to which a little bone meal has been added. Cushion plants that have become rather loose will make new growth if the top dressing is worked well into the plant.

Throughout the autumn care should be taken to remove falls of leaves that have settled on the rock garden, particularly around the autumn-flowering plants such as *Gentiana sino-ornata*.

Rock plants with felted or woolly leaves, such as *Raoulia australis*, may rot as a result of excessive wet in winter. These can be sheltered from rain by fixing a pane of glass above them, using supports of galvanized wire.

A rock garden will almost certainly contain a much wider selection of plants than any other feature of the garden. Many plants, including bulbs and deciduous herbaceous subjects, will have periods of dormancy when there will be no sign of their presence. These certainly should be labelled as should anything else that is in any way uncommon. Care with labelling as soon as plants are introduced to the garden is one of the first steps in building up knowledge about plants.

For those fascinated by alpine plants, an alpine house may be the next step. It has the great advantage of not needing any special heating and it is a pleasant place to work during the cold winter months and an ideal shelter for the temperamental plants which may not survive the unpredictable conditions in northern Europe as compared to their natural habitat.

Gentiana sino-ornata

HERBACEOUS AND SHRUBBY PLANTS

ACAENA Mostly native to New Zealand, these plants carpet any area, even in poor soil, paving stones or shady places. They must therefore be planted carefully or they will smother other rock plants.

A. microphylla, h. 2cm (1in), has tiny spines or burrs on the fruit which turn red to make a late summer and early autumn display of colour.

ACHILLEA These are easy sun-loving plants that are of value for their attractive silvery foliage and their flat flowerheads. The dwarf achilleas form rather compact mats of leaves and flower freely over a long period in summer. They are easily propagated by division; in order to keep them neat it is advisable to divide and replant after flowering every two or three years.

A. argentea, h. 10cm (4in), has bright silver foliage and pure white flowers.

A. clavenae, h. 15cm (6in), also has ferny silver leaves and large white flowers.

A. 'King Edward', h. 15cm (6in), is a particularly good dwarf hybrid, with grey-green foliage and sulphur-yellow flowers.

A. tomentosa, h. 15cm (6in), has deep green hairy leaves and bright yellow flowers.

AETHIONEMA These are small shrubby evergreen plants that are natives of the sunny dry conditions in the Mediterranean region. In the rock garden they do best in a sunny position in free-draining alkaline soil but they will tolerate neutral or slightly acid conditions. When well suited they are free-flowering over a long period in late spring and autumn. They can be raised from seed except in the case of the hybrid *A. 'Warley Rose'*, which must be propagated from cuttings.

A. grandiflorum, h. 30cm (12in), has grey-green leaves and produces a long display of soft pink flowers from May until August.

A. pulchellum, h. 15cm (6in), is rather like a more dwarf form of *A. grandiflorum* with flowers of a deeper colour.

A. 'Warley Rose', h. 15cm (6in), is a hybrid of exceptional merit. It has neat blue-grey leaves and over a long flowering season produces a profusion of rose-pink flowers.

Achillea growing from a rock crevice

ALCHEMILLA The alchemillas tend to be free-seeding plants and therefore need to be treated with caution in the rock garden. The lady's mantle (*A. mollis*) is a rather too coarse and luxuriant plant but some of the smaller species are easy herbaceous perennials that are useful more for their attractive foliage than for their inconspicuous flowers. They are tolerant of a wide range of soils and conditions.

A. alpina, h. 10cm (4in), forms neat tufts of leaves that are prettily silvered at the edges and underneath. The sprays of yellow-green flowers are borne in summer.

A. erythropoda is a similar plant with a reputation for being less invasive.

ALYSSUM The alyssums are among the easiest plants for a dry sunny position, tolerating a wide range of soils and giving a brilliant display of flowers in shades of yellow during mid- and late spring. They are widely planted, sometimes to excess, and can leave large uninteresting gaps when flowering is over. They are, nonetheless, useful plants, particularly for the person

Alyssum saxatile

Androsace pyrenaica

starting a rock garden. They can be raised from seed but selected forms will not come true and need to be propagated from cuttings. All alyssums should be trimmed after flowering.
A. saxatile, h. 15-30cm (6-12in), produces tufts of greyish leaves spreading to 30cm (12in) and masses of bright yellow flowers. Selected forms include: 'Citrinum', with lemon-yellow flowers; 'Compactum', a neat-growing plant; 'Dudley King', with buff-coloured flowers; and 'Plenum', a dense-flowering fully double form.

ANDROSACE

These include some of the choicest alpine plants but many are difficult to maintain in cultivation, even in alpine house conditions. There are, however, several species that can be grown satisfactorily in rock gardens and, often more successfully, in scree beds, provided the soil is free draining and plants are given some protection from excess moisture in winter.
A. carnea, h. 2-7cm (1-3in), forms a cushion of tiny leaves dotted in summer with pink flowers.
A. lanuginosa, h. 7cm (3in), is a silver-leaved trailing species that is particularly attractive when planted in a crevice. The pink flowers are borne in late summer.
A. primuloides (A. sarmentosa), h. 10cm (4in), is one of the easier androsaces. The rosettes of slightly hairy leaves form dense mats from which emerge stems bearing pink flowers. Named forms include 'Chumbyi' and 'Salmon's Variety'.
A. pyrenaica must be regarded as an alpine house plant, though the abundance of white and yellow flowers which cover the entire plant is worth the extra attention.

42

ANTENNARIA This genus includes a number of prostrate mat-forming plants but only one species is widely cultivated. *A. dioica* 'Rosea', h. 10cm (4in), makes a silvery mat of creeping stems and produces button-like heads of pink flowers in summer. It is a useful plant in paving and to combine with bulbs, the more vigorous of which can be planted to grow through the stems. The variety *A. d.* 'Minima' is a neat little plant with white flowers.

AQUILEGIA The dwarf columbines are sometimes not long-lived but are, nonetheless, attractive rock garden plants that are beautiful in leaf and flower. All can be raised easily from fresh seed; the freedom with which species hybridize makes it difficult to maintain pure stocks but the hybrids are generally no less beautiful than the species. They all flower in early summer and thrive in sunny or lightly shaded positions where the soil is well drained.
A. alpina, h. 30cm (12in), is the common species of the European Alps. The large blue flowers are handsome but this plant can look out of scale in the rock garden and seeds itself so freely that it becomes a nuisance.
A. bertolonii, h. 10cm (4in), is an easy and lovely plant with deep blue flowers and dark green leaves.
A. flabellata, a Japanese species, is most commonly seen in the form 'Nana Alba', h. 12.5cm (5in). This has blue-grey leaves and sturdy white flowers.
A. scopulorum, h. to 25cm (10in), is a plant from the Rocky Mountains that has prettily cut grey-green foliage and flowers varying in colour from pale to violet blue.

ARABIS Snow-in-summer (*A. caucasica*, formerly *A. albida*) is a rampant grower which is therefore not suitable for the small rock garden, although it can be useful as part of a large-scale semi-wild planting on a bank. There are, however, several small species for small scale gardening.
A. androsace, h. 2cm (1in), makes a tiny rosette that is covered in tiny flowers in early summer. It is a good subject for an alpine sink garden.
A. ferdinandii-coburgii 'Variegata', h. 7cm (3in), is chiefly of interest for its mats of green and white variegated foliage. The white flowers are sometimes removed to show the leaves to best advantage. Grow in gritty soil in full sun.

ARENARIA Among the arenarias there are a few quiet plants that are useful and easy to grow.
A. balearica, h. 2cm (1in), loves shade and damp and forms a creeping mat of bright green leaves studded with starry white flowers for several months in spring and summer.

Arabis (with alyssum in the background)

A. montana, h. 7cm (3in), is a more showy plant, forming mats of deep green leaves and in the first half of summer producing a sustained display of small white flowers. Its principal drawback is that patches of a plant sometimes die back.
A. purpurascens, h. 5cm (2in), forms low tufts and bears pink to purple flowers in summer.

ARMERIA
The thrifts are sun-loving plants, easy to grow in almost all soils that are free-draining. The grass-like leaves form dense tufts even when grown between slabs of paving. The flowers are borne in late spring and summer. Plants can be propagated from seed, cuttings or by division.
A. juniperifolia (*A. caespitosa*), h. 7cm (3in), is small enough for a trough garden and is a good scree plant. The pink flowers are almost stemless. In the form 'Bevan's Variety' they are a deep rose.
A. maritima, h. 20cm (8in), is widely distributed as a native plant in much of Europe. The flowers are normally pink but selected forms include: 'Alba', white; 'Bloodstone', dark red; and 'Vindictive', red.

ASTER
The dwarf asters, all with rather large daisy-like flowers, are beautiful and easy subjects for sunny positions. They are clump-forming plants that tend to become straggly and lose vigour if not divided every two or three years.

Armeria maritima

A. alpinus, h. 15cm (6in), is the common aster of the European Alps. The flowers, which appear in late spring, have an orange centre with rays varying in colour from white to purple. The darker forms, including 'Wargrave', are the most desirable.

A. tibeticus, h. 15cm (6in), is a similar plant to *A. alpinus* but the flowers, in profusion in early summer, are bright blue.

ASTILBE

These are moisture-loving plants that do best in fertile soil in light shade. They are good plants for the peat bed and are worth a specially managed corner of the rock garden. The finely cut leaves are attractive in their own right. However, it is the frothy flower spikes, borne from mid-summer, when many rock garden plants have finished flowering, that are their principal appeal. Plants should be divided every three or four years; division is the best means of propagation.

A. chinensis 'Pumila', h. 30cm (12in), has dark green deeply cut leaves and fluffy flowerheads of purplish-pink.

A. crispa, h. 15cm (6in), has lovely ferny foliage and short flower spikes, pink in the variety 'Perkeo'.

A. glaberrima, h. 10cm (4in), is a real miniature with fine leaves that are sometimes bronzed and flowers that are pink and cream.

Two excellent hybrids are 'Bronze Elegance', with handsome foliage and bright pink flowers, and 'Sprite', with a profusion of soft pink flowers.

Aster alpinus

AUBRIETA
Aubrietas like sun and lime and give a long and vivid display in spring. For a bold effect they are exceptionally valuable but they are not suitable for associating with choice rock garden plants. In order to keep aubrietas neat they should be cut back after flowering. Plants are easily raised from seed but selected colours must be propagated from cuttings or by division.

CALLUNA
The common ling, a plant of acid moorland, flowers in late summer and early autumn and for that reason alone can make a useful subject for the lime-free rock garden. Plants can be propagated from cuttings or by layering.
C. vulgaris, h. 10-60cm (4-24in), is variable in foliage and flower colour as well as in size. For the rock garden it is worth selecting the choicer dwarf forms, such as *C. v.* 'Foxii Nana', and those with foliage that take on rich shades of red, orange and bronze.

Aubrieta

Campanula carpatica

CAMPANULA
The campanulas form a large genus, which contains many valuable rock garden plants. A few of the dwarf species are demanding and most satisfactorily grown in an alpine house. However, many others, some of the most beautiful included, are easy plants and they sustain interest in the rock garden in summer just when the main flush of spring-flowering plants is over. The colour range is limited — generally shades of blue and white — but this is more than compensated for by the profusion of elegant flowers. Although campanulas need good drainage, they should have plenty of water in the growing season. Most species are easily raised from seed and propagated by division.

C. arvatica, h. 5cm (2in), is a mat-forming species that bears starry violet-blue or, in the albino form, white flowers. It needs free drainage and makes a good plant for a crevice.

C. barbata, h. 20cm (8in), is said to be a biennial but will last for several years. The stems bearing the hairy pale blue flowers rise from a flat rosette of light green leaves.

C. carpatica, h. 10-20cm (4-8in), is a name covering a group of plants, all of which are lovely and easy to grow. The plants make tufted clumps with trailing stems and the wide bell-shaped flowers are white or various shades of blue.

C. cochlearifolia (*C. pusilla*), h. 7cm (3in), spreads by underground runners, forming compact mats of neat leaves above which the pendant flowers hang on short stems. A lovely white form exists but generally flowers are in shades of blue.

C. garganica, h. 15cm (6in), gives a long display of starry blue flowers in late summer. It is an excellent plant for walls.

C. portenschlagiana (*C. muralis*), h. 10cm (4in), is a lovely plant that will thrive in light shade and full sun to produce a magnificent show of starry bells in late summer.

CASSIOPE
Lime-free soil and a lightly shaded cool position are essential for these evergreen members of the heather family. Some of the really dwarf species are difficult plants but those mentioned here are well suited in peat beds. Cassiopes are low-growing shrubby plants with wiry stems closely covered with tiny leaves. The small bell-like flowers are borne in late spring and early summer. Propagation is normally from soft cuttings taken in mid-summer. Any cassiope will benefit the rock garden provided you give it the correct care and conditions.

C. lycopodioides, h. 7cm (3in), a prostrate grower, is the easiest species and one of the best. It can spread as much as 45cm (18in). The pendant white flowers, which are borne in late spring, hang on wiry stems from mossy branches.

C. tetragona, h. 45cm (18in), is an erect shrublet with dark green foliage and white flowers that are sometimes tinged pink.

CELMISIA
Despite a reputation for being rather difficult, the New Zealand daisies are worth a place in the rock garden. They have striking white flowers with orange centres and the leaves are often covered on the reverse with silvery or white hairs. Celmisias prefer a slightly richer and moister soil than many rock garden plants and do best in light shade. Species with woolly leaves may need overhead protection in winter.

Celmisia coriacea

Propagation is generally from cuttings or by division.
C. argentea, h. 7cm (3in), makes stiff grey tufts with stemless flowers in early summer. It is a good plant for the trough garden.
C. bellidioides, h. 2cm (1in) is a moisture-loving species that forms close mats of dark green leaves. The flowers, borne in early summer, have bright orange centres.
C. coriacea, h. 30cm (12in), a particularly fine plant, has pointed silvery leaves; the flowers are borne in summer on sturdy silvery stems.

CHEIRANTHUS
The bedding wallflowers do not belong properly in the rock garden but there are dwarf forms that are reasonably long-lived and these are useful for their profuse display of fragrant flowers in early summer. They need poor rather than rich soil and an open position.
C. cheiri 'Harpur Crewe', h. 30cm (12in), is a sterile double yellow form that is very free-flowering. Increase from heeled cuttings.

CORYDALIS
Delicate ferny foliage and curiously tubular and lipped flowers are both attractive features of the plants in this genus. Plants are most satisfactorily increased from seed.

Cheiranthus cheiri 'Harpur Crewe'

C. cashmeriana, h. 15cm (6in), must count as one of the
treasures of the rock garden. It is not an easy plant, demanding
a cool, humid atmosphere and lime-free soil. However, the
flowers are of such unusual and beautiful colouring, brilliant
blue with a tinge of green, that it is hard to resist attempting it.
It flowers in late spring and early summer and there are odd
flowers later on.
C. cheilanthifolia, h. 20cm (8in), a yellow-flowered Chinese
species, it is easy-going provided it is given a sunny position. It
does not sow itself quite so freely as *C. lutea*.
C. lutea, h. 20cm (8in), is a common and easy plant that is a
great colonizer of walls. The yellow flowers are borne almost
continuously from spring to autumn. Beautiful though this
plant is and easily checked by weeding, it is too free-seeding to
associate with choice and rare plants.

CYTISUS

The brooms include some free-flowering shrubby
plants that are excellent for the medium to large rock garden.
They thrive in almost any soil provided that they have a sunny
well-drained spot. Species can be grown from seed but all can
be propagated from cuttings. None of them transplants well.
C. ardoinii, h. 15cm (6in), is a mat-forming species with a
spread of about 30cm (12in). Plants are covered with bright
yellow pea-like flowers in late spring.
C. beanii, h. 55cm (24in) and spread up to 80cm (36in), makes
a magnificent display of golden-yellow flowers in early
summer.
C. kewensis, h. 55cm (21in) and spread 120cm (48in), needs a
really large rock garden or a sunny bank. The pale yellow
flowers are produced in great profusion in late spring or early
summer.

DAPHNE

The hardy dwarf daphnes are among the most
valued shrubs for the rock garden. Most have pretty and
deliciously fragrant flowers and, although some are a great test
of the alpine gardener's skill, several are not so difficult. They
all like a sunny position but the roots should be given a cool
run, shaded by other plants or by large flat stones. Daphnes
may not prove long lived and they can be difficult to propagate
from cuttings. Layering is a slow but more reliable method.
D. arbuscula, h. 15cm (6in), a neat and sturdy evergreen plant,
produces terminal clusters of rosy flowers in mid-summer.
D. blagayana, h. 15cm (6in), can build up a spread of 150cm
(60in). It is evergreen but not a leafy plant. The sweetly scented
creamy flowers are borne in terminal heads in spring.
D. cneorum, h. 15cm (6in), a deservedly popular evergreen
species, makes twiggy growth and the densely clustered
fragrant flowers are borne in summer. The form *D. c.* 'Eximia'
is considered the best.

Cytisus kewensis and *C. praecox*
Daphne cneorum

52

DIANTHUS The perennial members of this genus are some
of the best-loved rock garden plants. They make tufty cushions
of evergreen leaves, frequently blue-grey in colour, and flower
generously in early summer, when spring plants have finished.
Many are strongly fragrant. All need a sunny position and good
drainage; an alkaline soil is not essential but many do well on
lime. Species and dwarf hybrids of dianthus are useful plants in
paving and in screes; some of the tiniest also make excellent
trough plants. Species can be raised from seed and all are
readily propagated from cuttings.

D. deltoides, the maiden pink, h. 25cm (10in), has narrow
green leaves and small flowers that are produced over a long
season in summer. It is worth searching out namcd forms, such
as 'Brilliant', bright pink; and 'Flashing Light', crimson.

D. freynii, h. 5cm (2in), is a species that is particularly suited to
growing in a scree bed. The leaves make a grey-green cushion
and the flowers are pink.

D. neglectus, h. 10-20cm (4-8in), is a lovely but variable plant,
the flowers ranging in colour from pale pink to bright crimson.
In all its forms the reverse of the petals is buff-coloured.

The miniature hybrids, h. to 15cm (6in), suitable for rock
gardens are numerous and the following is no more than a
selection for beginners: 'Dubarry', deep pink; 'Fanal', bright
pink; 'La Bourbrille', pink but also available in a white form;
'Little Jock', semi-double pink; and 'White Bouquet', white.

Dianthus 'Little Jock'

DICENTRA

The dicentras are graceful plants, producing arching sprays of hanging flowers in early summer. The fern-like foliage, which is often grey-green, dies down shortly after flowering but these plants are reliably perennial. Dicentras are not difficult, tolerating sun and part shade, but they need moist and reasonably rich soil. Propagate by division.

D. cucullaria, h. 15cm (6in), has pale green finely divided foliage and locket-like nodding flowers that are white tipped with yellow.

D. eximia, h. 30cm (12in), flowers throughout summer, the bright pink heart-shaped lockets being carried in nodding sprays over grey-green foliage.

DODECATHEON

The shooting stars, a North American genus, are moisture-loving plants best suited in a lightly shaded position. Stems emerge from a rosette of leaves to bear cyclamen-like flowers in summer; the leaves die down shortly after flowering is over. Propagate by division.

D. meadia, h. 30cm (12in), generally the most readily available of the shooting stars, has purple flowers with protruding yellow anthers.

D. pauciflorum, h. 20cm (8in), in size is the best suited species for the rock garden. The form 'Red Wings' has crimson flowers.

Dodecatheon pauciflorum

DRYAS
One shrubby evergreen species of this genus is a spectacular feature of the alpine flora of Europe, covering large areas with its large white flowers, which are followed later by feathery seedheads.

D. octopetala, h. 10cm (4in), makes wide mats of attractive leaves, sometimes as much as 60cm (24in) across. In cultivation it can flower rather sparsely; best results are achieved with gritty soil in a sunny position. It spreads its stems over the stones in the rock garden. A tiny version, *D. o.* 'Minor', is suitable for a trough garden.

EPIMEDIUM
The epimediums are highly regarded as ground-covering foliage plants. The dwarfer forms are delightful subjects for shady corners of the rock garden. The leaves, wonderfully fresh in spring, are almost evergreen and the sprays of flowers, although never showy, have an airy grace. Epimediums need moist peaty or leafy soil. Increase plants by division.

E. alpinum, h. 25cm (10in), has pretty toothed leaves and the flowers, borne in spring, are red and yellow.

E. grandiflorum (*E. macranthum*), h. 25cm (10in), varies from white to violet in flower colouring. The form 'Rose Queen' is a good deep pink.

E. rubrum, h. 30cm (12in), a crimson-flowered hybrid, has beautiful red-tinted foliage.

Dryas octopetala

ERICA The heathers are often considered inappropriate for the rock garden; all too commonly they are relegated to bleak expanses and left to themselves. Planted in moderation and with judicious selection of dwarf forms, they can make excellent rock garden subjects. They are easily propagated from cuttings and by layering.

E. carnea, h. 15-20cm (6-8in), provides the most suitable forms. It is a variable species and the range of named cultivars is vast. They are all winter flowering and, unlike many heathers, are tolerant of lime. The following is a limited selection: 'Eileen Porter', carmine flowers; 'Praecox Rubra', prostrate growth and deep pink flowers; 'Springwood Pink' and 'Springwood White', densely flowered forms with pink and white flowers respectively; 'Vivellii', dark foliage and crimson flowers; and 'Winter Beauty', compact growth and dark pink flowers.

ERODIUM They will thrive on almost any soil but do require sun. They enjoy a long flowering season which makes them ideal for the rock garden.

E. corsicum, h. 7cm (3in), is a mat-forming plant which is perfect for rock crevices. It may need to be given alpine house treatment in colder areas as it hates the wet winters. The silvery leaves offset the tiny rosettes of pink flowers whose petals are streaked with a deeper pink.

Erica carnea 'Springwood White'

GAULTHERIA
The gaultherias are hardy evergreen shrubby plants that bear modest urn-shaped flowers followed by attractive berries. They are plants for lightly shaded positions where the soil is moist and lime-free; they are well suited to planting in peat beds. Increase plants by taking cuttings.

G. miqueliana, h. 30cm (12in), may spread as much as 1m (40in). The small white flowers are borne in early summer; the white fruits that follow are frequently tinged pink.

G. procumbens, h. 15cm (6in), is another spreading species. It bears white or pinkish flowers followed by red berries.

GENISTA
Among the genistas are several dwarf shrubs that in a sunny well-drained position give a rich display of golden pea-shaped flowers in early summer. These plants may be short lived; they are all the better for a light and gritty soil. Propagate from cuttings. Genistas do not like being moved.

G. lydia, h. 75cm (30in), can spread as much as 150cm (60in). The arching branches are covered in flowers in late spring and early summer.

G. pilosa 'Prostrata', h. 7cm (3in), is a ground-hugging form with a spread of approximately 125cm (50in). The small yellow flowers are borne in great profusion in early summer.

G. sagittalis, h. 15cm (6in), has winged stems with a curious jointed appearance. The serried spikes of flowers are borne in mid-summer.

Gaultheria procumbens

GENTIANA   No group of plants is more firmly associated with mountains and alpine gardens than the gentians. The association has been fixed by the rare beauty of their gorgeous blue trumpet or starry flowers, although blue is not the only colour found in the genus. It must be admitted that some among them are the most tantalizing of alpines, promising a sumptuous display but proving shy when it comes to flowering.
G. acaulis, h. 7cm (3in), is the best known and most frustrating species of the genus. Mats of healthy deep green leaves will flourish in open positions where the soil is loamy. The mystery is why one clump will produce the deep blue short-stemmed trumpets, even in great profusion, while another clump, apparently thriving, will fail to flower. Plants should be divided and replanted every three or four years.
G. septemfida, h. 15cm (6in), an Asiatic species, is the easiest to grow successfully of all the commonly cultivated gentians. It is not fussy about soil but should be given an open sunny position. The best forms are deep blue with lighter markings inside the trumpets. It is a good idea to buy plants in flower to ensure that the colour is not muddy. Increase selected plants from cuttings.
G. sino-ornata, h. 10cm (4in), is a free-flowering Asiatic species if established in lime-free moist soil in light shade. The vivid blue of its flowers is one of the great joys of the autumn.
G. verna, h. 7cm (3in), a great beauty of the European Alps, has starry blue flowers in spring. It needs a gritty but quite rich soil and a position in full sun.

Genista pilosa

58

GERANIUM In the cranesbill family, which includes a number of perennial border plants of the first quality, there are fortunately several summer-flowering dwarf species of great merit. Most are clump-forming plants with attractive dissected leaves, easily grown in sunny positions where the soil is free draining. Plants can be propagated by division; many species are easily raised from seed.

G. argenteum, h. 15cm (6in), a good plant for the scree garden, has silvery foliage and pink flowers with deeper pink veining.

G. cinereum, h. 15cm (6in), is similar to *G. argenteum* but less silvery in leaf. The name 'Ballerina' has been given to what is probably a hybrid of *G. cinereum*. The flowers are soft pink with dark red veining.

G. dalmaticum, h. 10cm (4in), makes a neat clump of glossy green leaves, which colour well in autumn. The flowers, borne generously, are a clear pink.

G. farreri (*G. napuligerum*), h. 15cm (6in), is one of the finest species but it needs perfect drainage to thrive. The large pink flowers have prominent black anthers.

G. sanguineum lancastriense, h. 7cm (3in), is a spreading prostrate form that is easy to grow and gives pink flowers.

Geranium subcaulescens

Geranium sanguineum lancastriense

G. subcaulescens, h. 15cm (6in), sometimes considered a subspecies of *G. cinereum*, is distinguished by the vivid crimson of its flowers, intensified by a dark eye.
G. wallichianum 'Buxton's Blue', h. 20cm (8in), is a species that does well in light shade or full sun and has branching stems that thread their way innocently through other plants carrying, over a long season, soft blue flowers.

GEUM The geums are best known as border plants but they contain several good dwarf species. The flowers, like single roses, are borne in early summer. The two species mentioned are easy plants in sunny well-drained positions. Propagate by division.
G. borisii, h. 25cm (10in), has attractive foliage and showy flowers of vivid orange.
G. montanum, h. 25cm (10in), a native of the European Alps, makes neat clumps of hairy leaves and produces a long succession of yellow flowers.

GYPSOPHILA A few members of this genus are cushion-forming plants that do well in crevices or on the tops of walls.
G. repens, h. 10cm (4in), the most commonly available of the dwarf-growing species, is a lime-loving plant. It forms a dense bunch with trailing stems, having a spread of 12in (30cm). The flowering season lasts for several weeks in summer, colour, depending on form, varying from white to deep pink.

HEBE There is a lingering doubt about the hardiness of the shrubby veronicas from New Zealand. However, several dwarf species have come through harsh European winters unharmed. As most hebes are easily propagated from cuttings, their virtues should outweigh the disadvantage of marginal hardiness.

H. buchananii 'Minor', h. 10cm (4in), makes a tiny shrublet of wiry stems densely clothed in leaves. The white flowers are borne in mid-summer. This is a useful little plant for a trough garden.

H. 'Carl Teschner', h. 30cm (12in), is a fine hybrid plant with greyish leaves that makes a lovely mound of violet flowers over a longseason in summer.

H. 'Pagei', 25cm (10in), has attractive grey-green foliage outlined in red. Bluish-white flowers are borne in terminal clusters in mid-summer.

HELIANTHEMUM The rock rose is a native over most of Europe, often found thriving on chalk. It makes a shrubby spreading bush of lax growth.

H. nummularium, h. to 30cm (12in), is the parent of many cultivated forms, which vary to some extent in habit, foliage colour (some are beautifully silvery) and flower colour. In general, they are too vivid and vigorous to associate with small

Helianthemum nummularium

choice plants. Nonetheless, they are hard to equal for giving a broad effect in a grouping of easy-going plants. In a sunny position they flower prolifically over a long summer season. Later flowering is encouraged by trimming bushes after the first display. In any event, trimming is desirable to keep the shape of plants neat. Good named forms include: 'Ben Dearg', orange with dark centre; 'Ben Heckla', deep bronze; 'Sterntaler', yellow; 'The Bride', white; and 'Wisley Pink', soft pink. Propagate from heeled cuttings taken in summer.

HEPATICA

The hepaticas, closely related to the anemones (with which they were previously classified), are delightful spring-flowering woodland plants. They do best in a lightly shaded cool position where the soil is leafy. They are lovely plants for the peat bed. Hepaticas can be raised from seed or by division. However, clumps are slow to build up to a size that justifies being divided.

H. nobilis (*H. triloba*), h. 10cm (4in), has pretty three-lobed leaves and, typically, mauve flowers. Pink, white and double forms also occur and these are sometimes offered by specialist nurseries.

H. transsilvanica (*H. angulosa*), h. 15cm (6in), is like a larger form of *H. nobilis* but with downy and more rounded leaves. White and pink forms occur but normally the flowers are blue.

Hepatica transsilvanica

HYPERICUM

All the dwarf shrubby hypericums revel in a sunny position, where they will give a prolonged summer display of handsomely bossed golden flowers. Regrettably some of the really dwarf species are not reliably hardy; those mentioned are among the hardiest. Plants can be propagated from cuttings and from seed; look out for self-sown seedlings. They flower in the summer and early autumn.

H. coris, h. 15cm (6in), is an evergreen shrublet of upright growth and heather-like foliage. It is hardiest in well-drained and rather poor soil. The golden flowers are borne in mid-summer.

H. olympicum, h. 25cm (10in), is a beautiful and easy plant. It makes a rounded bush of grey-green foliage, which is smothered by large golden flowers over a long season. A particularly lovely form, *H. o.* 'Citrinum', has pale yellow flowers. *H. polyphyllum* is difficult to distinguish in cultivation from *H. olympicum*. A good pale form, 'Sulphureum', is sometimes listed.

Hypericum olympicum 'Citrinum'

H. reptans, h. 7cm (3in), makes a neat mat of light green leaves, which take on attractive warm colouring in autumn. The flowers, which are reddish in bud, open to yellow.
H. rhodopeum, h. 15cm (6in), a lax-growing species with grey-green foliage, is an inoffensive spreader that gives a long display of large golden flowers.
H. tricocaulon is a neat prostrate grower. The buds are crimson but open to reveal bright yellow flowers.

IBERIS
The candytufts cannot be considered plants of great refinement but they are among the most reliable of rock garden plants, providing a bold splash of white in spring and early summer. They are best associated with other easy-going plants in a sunny well-drained position. Propagate from softwood cuttings.
I. saxatilis, h. 10cm (4in), an evergreen prostrate shrublet, is a useful little plant for growing in a scree bed. It gives a generous display of small white flowers in early summer.
I. sempervirens, h. 45cm (18in), the parent of the main cultivated forms of the perennial candytuft, is a free-flowering shrubby evergreen. The form 'Little Gem', h. 25cm (10in), has the advantage of making a neat squat plant but 'Snowflake' makes the boldest display of large white flowers.

LEONTOPODIUM
Despite a reputation for being one of the difficult plants of the high Alps, the edelweiss is in reality a reasonably accommodating subject provided it is given good drainage and an open position. It is included here on account of its status as a representative alpine — the traditional alpine — and as a curiosity rather than because it is a plant of remarkable beauty.
L. alpinum, h. 15cm (6in), a plant of woolly grey-green leaves, produces flat flowerheads in spring. The asymmetrical star shapes are formed by the bracts; the clusters of daisy flowers have no rays.

LEUCANTHEMUM
This is a hardy, sub-shrubby species from North Africa which needs full sun in a warm position.
L. hosmariense, h. 15-20cm (6-8in), spread 30cm (12in), has daisy-like white flowers which appear in succession during the summer months. The leaves are silvery on woody stems.

LEWISIA
This North American genus provides the rock garden with many outstanding plants. They make rosettes of thick succulent leaves (which in many species are evergreen) and, in early summer, bear showy sprays of flowers, generally in a colour range from pink to orange. They require very good

drainage, though not thin soil, and an open sunny position.
Many appear to be intolerant of lime. They do well planted on
their sides in crevices. Where there is any risk of winter wet
there should be a liberal layer of chippings around the necks of
plants. Lewisias, which hybridize freely, grow readily from
seed.

L. brachycalyx, h. 7cm (3in), an evergreen species, has greyish
leaves with a spread of 20cm (8in). The white or pinkish-white
flowers are borne singly in late spring.

L. cotyledon, h. 30cm (12in), is the parent of many attractively
coloured forms and has played a major part in the breeding of
hybrids. Flower colour varies from white to apricot.

L. tweedyi, h. 15cm (6in), an evergreen and generally
considered the pick of the species, forms clumps of tough
leaves and produces many stems, each bearing a single large
flower of pink lusciously suffused with apricot. In
nurserymen's lists the hybrids, in most cases plants with the
virtues of their parents magnified, have displaced the true
species. Look out for 'George Henley', 'Paula', 'Pinkie' and
'Rose Splendour'.

LINUM The perennial and sub-shrubby flaxes are bright and
easy plants, not fussy about soil, that will thrive in sunny
positions. They can be propagated from cuttings and are easily
raised from seed.

Lewisia cotyledon

L. arboreum, h. 30cm (12in), should be given alpine house treatment in cold areas. The flowers are creamy or bright yellow with white petals.

L. flavum, h. 40cm (15in), a hardy species with grey-green leaves, makes a fine display of golden flowers over a long season in summer.

L. monogynum, h. 30cm (12in), has large white blossoms on short, leafy stems in summer.

L. narbonense, h. 45cm (18in), may be considered too tall for many rock gardens. However, its prolonged display of rich blue flowers throughout summer makes it a good background plant.

LITHOSPERMUM
This genus contains several mat-forming shrubby and perennial plants remarkable for their long display of rich blue flowers. They are not difficult in sunny positions but the most common species, *L. diffusum*, and the forms derived from it are lime-haters. Plants are best increased from soft cuttings.

L. diffusum, h. 10cm (4in) and spread 55cm (21in), is a plant of great beauty. The blue of the flowers has a gentian-like intensity and in the form of 'Heavenly Blue' they are borne generously from early summer throughout a long season.

L. oleifolium, h. 15cm (6in), spreads less widely than *L. diffusum*. The sky-blue flowers are flushed pink in the bud.

Linum narbonense

Oenothera missouriensis

OENOTHERA The evening primroses include a few truly dwarf species and others of sprawling growth that are easily accommodated in the rock garden. They are rather coarsely lush plants, usually not long lived, that flower freely in summer. As the common name suggests, in most species the flowers, which are wide funnels, open in the evening. Oenotheras need a sunny position with good drainage. However, they should have a plentiful supply of water in the summer months. In late autumn cut plants down to ground level. The species grow readily from seed.

O. acaulis, h. 15cm (6in), is generally treated as a biennial. The broad white flowers, which turn to pink as they age, are carried at ground level over dandelion-like leaves.

O. missouriensis, h. 15cm (6in), is a floppy trailing species with a spread of 45cm (18in). The huge yellow flowers, marked red in the bud, are borne over a long summer season, each flower persisting for several days.

PAPAVER The dwarf poppies are delightful rock garden plants, their bright crinkled flowers appearing in long succession throughout the summer. They are rather short lived but their capacity to self-seed ensures that colonies persist. They need sun and good drainage but otherwise are easily satisfied. Poppies do not transplant well so the seed should be sown where the plants are to grow.

P. alpinum, h. 10cm (4in), has pretty grey-green ferny leaves and the flowers are white, pink, yellow and orange. Several closely related species, sometimes considered as subspecies, are also occasionally available. These include: *P. kerneri*, yellow; *P. pyrenaicum* and *P. rhaeticum*, variable; and *P. sendtneri*, white.

P. miyabeanum, h. 10cm (4in), a Japanese plant, is similar to the European alpine species but has a reputation for being longer lived.

PENSTEMON
The North American alpine penstemons are a numerous group of sub-shrubs with showy snapdragon-like flowers. They are intolerant of wet conditions, requiring sunny positions and gritty soil. They often prove short lived but are easily propagated from cuttings; their qualities justify maintaining a stock of young plants.

P. davidsonii, h. 10cm (4in), is a low spreading shrublet, producing short racemes of ruby-red flowers in late spring and early summer.

P. heterophyllus, h. 30cm (12in), has grey-green leaves and sends up spikes of flowers that are blue tinged with pink. 'True Blue' is a lovely pure blue form.

Papaver alpinum

Penstemon newberryi

P. menziesii, h. 25cm (10in), a semi-erect shrub with small toothed leaves, has purplish flowers in mid-summer.

P. newberryi, h. 30cm (12in), is similar to *P. menziesii* but the flowers are purplish-pink.

P. pinifolius, h. 15cm (6in), has distinctive needle-like leaves and narrow flowers that are orange-red.

P. roezlii, h. 25cm (10in), one of the loveliest of the penstemons, forms a loose mound that in mid-summer is covered with rich red flowers.

P. scouleri, h. 30cm (12in), close in general appearance to *P. menziesii*, is one of the easiest and gives a prolific summer display of lilac flowers.

PHLOX The shrubby and dwarf phloxes, North American plants in origin, are a valuable group for the rock garden. They form mats of rather narrow leaves and bear dense clusters of bright flowers in spring and early summer. They thrive in sunny well-drained positions. If plants become straggly they should be trimmed after flowering.

P. douglasii, h. 10cm (4in), is a profusely flowering prostrate species with many excellent named forms. These include: 'Boothman's Variety', mauve; 'Eva', pink with a darker eye; and 'Snow Queen', pure white.

P. subulata, h. 10cm (4in), creates lovely broad effects in a

Phlox subulata

group of easy-going plants, taking over as the aubrietas finish. This spreading species benefits particularly from trimming when flowering is over. Among the cultivated forms of good colour are the following: 'Betty', salmon-pink; 'Bonita', lavender; 'Sensation', deep pink; and 'Temiscaming', brilliant crimson.

POTENTILLA
One at least of the dwarf potentillas, *P. nitida*, is a rock garden plant of quality and others are useful for their succession of saucer-shaped flowers throughout summer. They are sun-lovers and, although not fussy about soil, need good drainage. Propagation is by division and from cuttings.

P. aurea, h. 15cm (6in), which makes small mounds of shiny green foliage, has deep yellow flowers, double in the form *P. a.* 'Plena'.

P. crantzii, h. 15cm (6in), is an erect sub-shrub with the yellow flowers so typical of many of the cinquefoils (compound leaf of five leaflets).

P. megalantha (*P. fragiformis*), h. 20cm (8in), has large deep green hairy leaves and handsome yellow flowers.

P. nitida, h. 15cm (6in), makes lovely silvery mats and bears large almost stemless flowers that can range in colour from near white to rose-red. It flowers best in gritty rather thin soil.

Primula frondosa

PRIMULA The primulas constitute an enormous family
containing numerous American, Asiatic and European plants
of the first quality. Of those sufficiently dwarf for the rock
garden, a number are rather tricky alpines, rewarding for the
specialist but not easy to grow to perfection in the open garden.
Nonetheless, there are still many species and cultivated forms
of great beauty that are not difficult to grow. In very broad
terms it can be said that the plants that are suited to being
grown in the rock garden prefer an open sunny or lightly
shaded position, soil that is well drained but reasonably rich in
humus, and a plentiful supply of moisture. Propagate from seed
or by division.

P. edgeworthii (*P. winteri*), h. 10cm (4in), a lovely Himalayan
species, may need protection from excessive winter damp but
is one of the easier Asiatic species. The grey-green leaves are
well covered in farina and the flowers, which begin to appear
in mid-winter, are mauve with a pale eye.

P. farinosa, h. 15cm (6in), a European species that has a wide
natural distribution, has silvery leaves and yellow-centred pink
flowers in early spring.

P. frondosa, h. 15cm (6in), is like a stouter form of *P. farinosa*.

P. juliae, h. 7cm (3in), a pretty mat-forming plant with
yellow-centred purplish flowers, has been largely displaced by
the hybrids, such as 'Wanda', derived from it. These are
frequently grouped under the name *P. juliana*.

P. marginata, h. 10cm (4in), a species with silvery leaves that
are heavily powdered, bears heads of lavender-blue flowers in
mid-spring. 'Linda Pope' is a choice form.

P. pubescens, h. 10cm (4in), covers a number of hybrids between *P. auricula* and, particularly, *P. rubra*. Good forms include 'Argus', purple with white centres; 'Faldonside', crimson; 'Harlow Car', cream; and 'Rufus', brick red.
P. rosea, h. 15cm (6in), a fine pond-side plant for the rock garden, makes a bold display in early spring with deep pink flowers. 'Visser de Greer' is an exceptional selection.

PULSATILLA
The pulsatillas, closely allied to the anemones (with which they were formerly classified), are attractive for their hairy and ferny foliage, their silky cup-shaped flowers and their feathery seedheads. They are lime-lovers that are easy in sunny well-drained positions. Propagate from fresh seed.
P. alpina, h. 30cm (12in), a white-flowered pulsatilla, is commonly represented in cultivation by the handsome yellow-flowered form 'Sulphurea'.
P. vulgaris, the pasque flower, h. 30cm (12in), although on the tall side, must rank as one of the most desirable of the easy rock garden plants. The common form is mauve but the colour range is from white to deep red.

Pulsatilla vulgaris

72

RAMONDA This small genus provides plants that are ideal for the shady side of rock walls. They form rosettes of hairy evergreen leaves and in mid to late spring bear saucer-shaped flowers. An advantage of planting them in a vertical crevice is that moisture cannot collect in the rosette; the roots, however, should be bedded in a reasonably moisture-retentive soil in which leaf mould or peat has been incorporated. Plants are long lived and show remarkable recuperative powers, even when the leaves have shrivelled, after drought. Propagate from leaf cuttings or increase from seed.

R. myconii, h. 15cm (6in), the most readily available species, has mauve flowers with conspicuous golden stamens. A number of named forms are available, including 'Alba' which is pure white.

R. serbica, h. 10cm (4in), is like a more compact form of *R. myconii* except that the anthers are purple not golden.

RAOULIA The raoulias, mainly from New Zealand, build up tight hummocks or mats of tiny rosettes. In many species the miniature flowers appear as a stain on the silvery or grey-green foliage. Those that are suitable for cultivation

Ramonda myconii

outdoors need gritty soil, full sun and preferably some overhead protection in winter. Propagate by division.

R. australis, 1cm (½in), makes a beautiful silvery mat with a spread of up to 30cm (12in). It is yellowed in summer by the flowers.

R. lutescens, h. 1cm (½in), is like a crusted grey-green carpet spreading as much as 45cm (18in), which is covered in summer with lemon-yellow flowers.

RHODODENDRON
This vast genus, so rich in evergreen and deciduous plants, includes many dwarf and prostrate species and hybrids. They provide some of the best small shrubs for the rock garden or peat bed wherever the soil is lime-free. As a rule, they are not temperamental plants but, in addition to an acid soil, they require a plentiful supply of moisture, protection from cold winds and a position shaded from early morning sun — rapid thawing of frosted blossoms can cause more damage than frost itself. Provided these conditions are met, they are not as demanding of shade as is commonly thought and often flower better in open positions. Propagation is generally from cuttings or by layering. The following selection is confined to evergreen species but many excellent hybrids are also available.

R. campylogynum, h. 30cm (12in), a species with glossy dark leaves, bears clusters of three or four waxy bells in shades of purple in late spring.

R. fastigiatum, h. to 75cm (30in), is a twiggy shrub that may eventually grow too large for the rock garden. The foliage is grey-green and the lavender-blue flowers are borne in mid-spring.

R. forrestii repens, h. 25cm (10in), a creeping shrub with a spread up to 125cm (50in), has leaves with a purple reverse and in mid-spring bears crimson flowers that are solitary or in pairs.

R. hanceanum nanum, h. 45cm (18in), has dark green leaves and pale yellow flowers carried in large clusters in early spring.

R. impeditum, h. 45cm (18in), is a variable densely twiggy shrub that flowers in late spring. The colour range is from mauve to blue.

R. radicans, h. 10cm (4in), one of the smallest species, is a tight prostrate plant with glossy dark green leaves. It bears solitary purplish flowers at the end of stems in late spring.

R. sargentianum, h. 55cm (21in), an aromatic plant, has glossy leaves and, once mature, bears large clusters of narrow yellow flowers in late spring.

SANGUINARIA
This genus contains a single species, which is easily grown in well-drained soil in sun or light shade. Propagation is by division.

Sanguinaria canadensis

S. canadensis, h. 30cm (12in), owes its common name, blood-root, to the red sap that exudes from damaged roots. The beautiful lobed grey-green leaves emerge in spring, temporarily enclosing the pure white anemone-like flowers. The double form, 'Flore Plena', is even more dazzling.

SAXIFRAGA

The huge saxifrage genus is one of the most important for the rock garden enthusiast. There are many species, forms and hybrids of such variety that 16 main sections have been recognized. Those listed, a tiny selection, need sharply drained soil, preferably containing lime, and an open position. Many are suited to planting in rocky crevices or in screes and the real miniatures are excellent in sinks. Propagation is by division.

S. aizoon (*S. paniculata*), h. 15cm (6in), a widely distributed and variable species, forms rosettes of narrow leaves encrusted with chalk. The sprays of flowers are generally white but there are pink and yellow forms. *S.* 'Whitehill' is a reliable and neat encrusted hybrid with *S. aizoon* as a likely parent. The flowers are creamy.

S. apiculata, h. 10cm (4in), probably a hybrid of the important Kabschia section, forms spreading mats of deep green leaves and bears yellow flowers in early spring. 'Alba' is a fine white form.

S. burseriana, h. 5cm (2in), forms dense cushions of blue-grey leaves and bears many stems of large white flowers in early spring. Named forms include 'Brookside', 'Gloria', both larger than the type, and 'Major Lutea', yellow.

S. cochlearis, h. 20cm (8in), makes tight mounds of silvery rosettes which produce sprays of white flowers in mid-summer. *S. c.* 'Minor' is a useful compact form.

S. cotyledon, h. to 60cm (24in), has lime-encrusted leaves forming symmetrical rosettes; it carries splendid sprays of white flowers in summer. The form 'Southside Seedling', with red flecking on the flowers, is outstanding.

S. jenkinsae, h. 2cm (1in), forms a dense cushion of grey-green leaves and produces a prolific display of pale pink flowers in early spring.

S. longifolia, h. 45cm (18in), makes handsome symmetrical grey-green rosettes and in summer sends up arching sprays of white flowers. It may take several years to flower and generally dies after flowering. 'Tumbling Waters' is a fine form.

S. moschata, h. 2-7cm (1-3in), covers a large group of saxifrages, all of which make mossy hummocks and bear sprays of, generally, creamy-yellow flowers on wiry stems. Named forms include: 'Atropurpurea', with red flowers, and 'Cloth of Gold', with yellow foliage and white flowers. The mossy hybrid *S.* 'Pixie' is a choice red-flowered compact plant.

Saxifraga 'Whitehill'

SEDUM
This large genus contains many easy sun-loving plants that may not rank among the first for beauty but are, nonetheless, useful sprawlers. They will often grow where much else fails. The leaves are rather succulent and there is a generous display of starry flowers. They self-propagate readily from seed and by layering; plants can be started from the leaves of succulent species.

S. acre, stonecrop, h. 5cm (2in), is a widespread species with a prodigious will to survive. The yellow flowers are borne over a long season in summer. *S. a.* 'Aureum' has bright yellow shoots in spring.

S. cauticolum, h. 15cm (6in), a deciduous species, produces heads of rosy red flowers in autumn.

S. spathulifolium, h. 10cm (4in), makes an evergreen hummock that sometimes takes a red tinge. The yellow flowers appear in early summer. 'Capablanca' is a form with almost white foliage.

SEMPERVIVUM
Much of the appeal of the sempervivums lies in the colouring and texture of the fleshy symmetrical rosettes and the cushion-forming habit. They can, however, be striking plants when they flower — stout stalks rising from the rosettes in summer to carry heads of yellow to red stars. After flowering the rosette shrivels away. Sempervivums enjoy full

Sedums and sempervivums

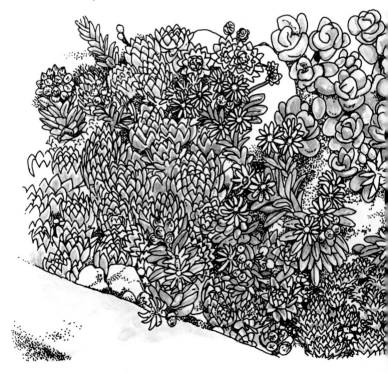

sun and gritty sharp-draining soil. Some species benefit from overhead protection in winter. Propagate from offsets.

S. arachnoideum, h. 10cm (4in), forms tight rounded rosettes in which the leaf tips are connected by a web of white hairs. Flowers are rose red.

S. montanum, h. 2cm (1in), is a common but variable alpine species. The mid-green leaves are covered in fine hairs and the flowers are purplish.

S. octopodes, h. 2cm (1in), throws out numerous stolons with offsets from its hairy rosettes. Flowers are greenish-yellow.

S. tectorum, the common houseleek, h. 7cm (3in), is an enormously variable species but generally has mid-green leaves tipped with maroon and purplish flowers. 'Calcareum' is a handsomely coloured form.

SISYRINCHIUM

The popular name blue-eyed grass accurately conveys the appearance of the commonest of these herbaceous perennials. They are plants for sunny positions where the soil is well drained but reasonably rich in humus. Propagation is by division.

S. angustifolium, h. 15cm (6in), forms iris-like clumps of leaves, which carry bright blue flowers in summer.

S. bermudiana, h. 25cm (10in), is like a larger form of *S. angustifolium* but with yellow at the base of the flowers.

SOLDANELLA All the soldanellas are remarkably similar in appearance, having dark green rounded leaves, slender stems and pretty bell flowers with fringed petals. They are humus-loving plants for cool, lightly shaded positions; they need particular protection from slugs. Propagation is from cuttings or by division.

S. alpina, h. to 15cm (6in), slowly builds up mats of kidney-shaped leaves and bears mauve flowers in spring, though sometimes rather sparsely in cultivation.

S. montana, h. 20cm (8in), is like a stouter form of *S. alpina* and flowers more freely.

VERONICA The shrubby veronicas from New Zealand have now been listed under *Hebe* but this still leaves a genus with many prostrate and dwarf species. They are invaluable in the rock garden for their spikes of blue, purple and white flowers in summer. All those listed are easy plants for sunny well-drained positions. Propagation is by division or from cuttings.

V. cinerea, h. 10cm (4in), forms mats of soft grey foliage and in summer gives a long display of violet-blue flowers.

V. prostrata, h. 15cm (6in), a mat-forming species with toothed mid-green leaves, is a lovely and easy rock garden plant. The flowers, borne over a long period, are deep blue. Named forms

Soldanella alpina

include: 'Pygmaea', very dwarf, and 'Rosea', with deep pink flowers.

V. teucrium, h. 20-30cm (8-12in), is a variable species but the dwarfer forms, making hummocky clumps, are valuable for their long display of sky-blue flowers in the second half of summer.

VIOLA

VIOLA Most of the highly cultivated pansies and violas, beautiful though they are, look out of place in the rock garden. However, there are numerous charming species that are easy to grow in an open or lightly shaded corner. They can be somewhat short lived but almost all self-seed freely. Plants can also be propagated from cuttings.

V. biflora, h. 7cm (3in), a widely distributed species, has fresh green kidney-shaped leaves and bright yellow flowers with fine brown veining over a long summer season.

V. labradorica 'Purpurea', h. 10cm (4in), is a particularly good plant in shade. The leaves are tinged purple and the flowers, borne in early summer, are mauve.

V. tricolor, heartsease, h. 10cm (4in), occurs wild over a wide area and is very variable. Its spreading stems bear pansy-like flowers over a long season in summer. Colour ranges from cream and yellow through blue to purplish-black and many bicolors.

Veronica prostrata

BULBOUS PLANTS

As in most gardening catalogues, the term 'bulb' is used rather loosely here to include those plants that grow from corms, tubers or rhizomes as well as true bulbs. It is a large category of garden plants including dwarf subjects that are invaluable in the rock garden.

ALLIUM Among the members of the onion family there are a number of attractive ornamental plants, although few of them are strikingly showy. Those mentioned thrive in sunny well-drained positions. Alliums can be propagated from seed, from bulbils or, in the case of species with rhizomatous roots, by division.

A. amabile, h. 15cm (6in), which has a rhizomatous root, produces a loose head of up to six small purplish flowers in late summer. *A. mairei* is similar.

A. beesianum, h. 25cm (10in), which also has a rhizomatous root, has hanging bell-like blue flowers in mid-summer.

A. cyaneum, h. 15cm (6in), another rhizomatous species and one of the most desirable alliums, produces small heads of

Allium narcissiflorum

Chionodoxa luciliae

upright blue flowers in mid-summer.
A. narcissiflorum, h. 20cm (8in), a rhizomatous species, is one
of the best for the rock garden. The hanging bell-shaped
flowers, which are borne in mid-summer, are pink to purple.

CHIONODOXA This small group of similar species
contains attractive early spring bulbs with bright starry blue
flowers. They are easily grown in sunny positions, provided the
soil is well drained, and if left undisturbed will gradually build
up to sizeable colonies.
C. gigantea, h. 15cm (6in), has violet-blue flowers with white
centres and is the largest flowered of the species.
C. luciliae, h. 15cm (6in), is the most readily available and an
excellent rock garden plant. The flowers are bright blue and
have a white centre. Pink forms are also in cultivation.

CROCUS No rock garden would be complete without a
planting of crocuses, a large genus of truly dwarf bulbs that are
marvellously varied in colour and markings. There are
autumn-, winter- and spring-flowering species, many of which
are easy to cultivate in a wide range of soils provided they get

the sun and there is good drainage. The large Dutch crocuses generally look out of place in a small rock garden.

C. chrysanthus, h. 7cm (3in), flowers in late winter and early spring. This species is best known for the excellent varieties and hybrids that have been produced from it. These include: 'Advance', yellow and bronze; 'Blue Pearl', blue with yellow centre; 'Goldilocks', yellow with purple base; 'Ladykiller', purple with white inside; 'Princess Beatrix', blue with golden base; and 'Zwanenburg Bronze', bronze and yellow.

C. tomasinianus, 7cm (3in), another easy species, flowers in late winter or early spring in varying shades of mauve.

CYCLAMEN

The hardy dwarf cyclamen are among the loveliest plants for the rock garden, pleasing as much by their handsomely marked leaves as by their elegant flowers. They thrive in full sun or part shade where the soil is free draining and are tolerant of lime. The dry corms may take a year or so to settle down but once established they are long lived.

C. coum, h. 7cm (3in), which flowers in winter and early spring, has rounded leaves that are sometimes silvered. The dumpy flowers are white, pink or carmine.

C. hederifolium (*C. neapolitanum*), h. 10cm (4in), an autumn-flowering species, deserves its popularity as a beautiful and easy plant. The flowers are white to carmine and the leaves heavily marbled.

ERYTHRONIUM

The peat garden or a cool, lightly shaded corner in the rock garden where there is plenty of leaf mould or peat are well suited to these exceptionally beautiful bulbs. They all flower mid to late spring; the nodding flowers have elegantly reflexed petals.

E. revolutum, h. 30cm (12in), has lightly mottled foliage and rose-pink flowers.

E. tuolumnense, h. 25cm (10in), produces bright green leaves and yellow flowers with greenish centres. Hybrids that are available include: 'Kondo', 'Pagoda' (both yellow) and 'White Beauty'.

GALANTHUS

The snowdrops are a remarkably homogeneous group of bulbs with characteristic drooping flowers consisting of three short inner petals with green markings and three long outer ones, normally without markings. They do well in the rock garden provided the soil is reasonably moist. Snowdrops are moved most satisfactorily while still in leaf, immediately after flowering.

G. nivalis, the common snowdrop, h. 10-20cm (4-8in), is a variable species but in all its forms it is a good rock garden plant.

Cyclamen hederifolium
Galanthus nivalis

IRIS The large iris genus includes a group of exceptionally lovely dwarf hardy species that make first-rate rock garden subjects. These reticulata irises (the name refers to the netting that surrounds the bulb) flower in late winter or early spring and, despite their fragile appearance, stand up well to frost and snow. They should be planted in open sunny positions with good drainage, preferably in soil containing some lime.

I. danfordiae, h. 10cm (4in), is one of the earliest of this group to come out, often pushing its greenish-yellow flowers through snow.

I. histrioides 'Major', h. 10cm (4in), produces sturdy flowers very early in the year, intense blue in colour with an orange crest.

I. innominata, h. 20cm (8in), flowers in late spring and early summer in variable shades of yellow. The plant forms in large clumps and prefers to be planted in a sunny place.

I. reticulata, h. 15cm (6in), is an easy and justly popular species. The form that is commonly available is deep blue with orange on the falls. Named forms include: 'Cantab', light blue; 'J.S. Dijt', purplish-red; and 'Royal Blue', deep blue.

LEUCOJUM The snowflakes, although superficially similar to snowdrops, are easily distinguished by the fact that all six petals are of the same size.

Iris innominata

L. autumnale, h. 25cm (10in), is best planted in a sunny position. The flowers, white tinged with pink, are borne on slender stems in early autumn.

L. vernum, h. 20cm (8in), has strap-like green leaves and produces its white flowers in early spring. It does best in a pocket of moist soil and will tolerate light shade.

MUSCARI

The grape hyacinths are excellent spring-flowering bulbs for the rock garden, easy to grow in all soils and positions. They make clumps of fleshy linear leaves, from which emerge leafless stems bearing crowded spikes of small, rounded and generally blue flowers. However, the common grape hyacinth (*M. neglectum, M. racemosum*), although popular and widely available, is too vigorous for the rock garden.

M. armeniacum, h. 25cm (10in), flowers in mid-spring; the deep-blue flowers have a white rim. 'Heavenly Blue' is a named form of particularly bright colouring.

M. botryoides, h. 20cm (8in), which flowers mid to late spring, is normally sky-blue but a desirable white form, 'Album', is also available.

M. tubergenianum, h. 20cm (8in) is an early spring bulb of great merit. The top flowers in the spike are dark blue, the lower ones open pale blue.

Muscari botryoides

NARCISSUS The *Narcissus* genus provides the gardener
with some of the best spring-flowering bulbs, including many
that are excellent plants for the rock garden. As well as the
delightful dwarf species, there are numerous short-growing
hybrids that do not look out of scale among other rock garden
plants. Bulbs should be planted as soon as they become
available in autumn. They are tolerant of a wide range of soils,
including chalk, but show a preference for reasonably moist
conditions.

N. cyclamineus, h. 20cm (8in), begins flowering in late winter.
The narrow trumpets and the swept-back petals, which give
the flowers a cyclamen-like shape, are the same deep yellow.

N. triandrus, the angel's tears daffodil, h. to 25cm (10in), is a
lovely plant with generally two or three cream or pale yellow
flowers to a stem in mid-spring.

The following, most early-spring flowering, are a few among
the many hybrids suitable for rock gardens: 'Baby Moon', h.
20cm (8in), many bright yellow sweetly scented flowers to a

Narcissus 'Jack Snipe'

Tulipa kaufmanniana

stem; 'Beryl', h. 20cm (8in), cream petals and orange cup; 'Jack
Snipe', h. 20cm (8in), slightly reflexed cream petals and a
primrose trumpet; and 'Tête-à-Tête', h. 20cm (8in), two or
more yellow trumpets to a stem.

SCILLA
The scillas, a large genus, are generally represented
in European gardens by two invaluable dwarf species that are
fully hardy and free flowering. Both are easy plants provided
they are given a sunny position in free-draining soil.
S. sibirica, h. 10cm (4in), produces several flower stems per
bulb, each bearing in early spring three or four nodding flowers
of brilliant blue. 'Spring Beauty' is a choice named form.
S. tubergeniana, h. 12cm (5in), is similar to *S. sibirica* but has
pale flowers with a dark stripe.

TULIPA
Tulips are indispensable spring-flowering bulbs but
many are too tall for rock gardens and their vivid colours can
be difficult to place. Bulbs should be planted late in autumn in
sunny well-drained positions. Some will settle down and
flower for a number of years but bulbs are generally lifted in
mid-summer, after the leaves have died down.
T. greigii, h. to 25cm (10in), is another species with vivid
scarlet flowers in mid-spring but remarkable also for the
handsome purplish mottling of the leaves. It has played an
important part in the breeding of many fine hybrids.
T. kaufmanniana, the water-lily tulip, h. 20cm (8in), flowers in
early spring, the wild form having creamy flowers tinged pink.
Some of the best dwarf varieties and hybrids have been derived
from it. These include 'Giuseppe Verdi', red and yellow.

DWARF CONIFERS

Although they can easily be overdone, dwarf conifers are useful plants for the rock garden, giving an established look and providing continuity throughout the seasons. In foliage colouring and texture as well as in form they are enormously varied and the range available is vast.

The following is a beginner's selection, which could easily be expanded by reference to the catalogues of specialist nurseries. Dwarf conifers are hardy plants and not demanding although they prefer being planted in open positions. An annual feed of a slow-release fertilizer forked in around plants is advisable. Starved plants are likely to lose foliage colour. The height given is only an approximate indication of ultimate size. Most of these cultivars are very slow growing and are unlikely to be much more than half the stated size after ten or twelve years.

CHAMAECYPARIS The false cypresses have produced a number of dwarf forms with distinctive foliage and colouring. *C. lawsoniana* 'Minima Aurea', h. 1.5m (60in), deserves its popularity as a rock garden plant. The foliage is bright yellow

and is slightly twisted. This form is very slow growing and at ten years is unlikely to be more than 30cm (12in). *C. l.* 'Minima Glauca' is similar in growth but has blue-green foliage.
C. obtusa 'Nana', h. 50cm (20in), is another slow-growing plant of spreading habit with dark green foliage.

CRYPTOMERIA
Many of the dwarf forms of the Japanese cedar associate well with heathers but probably grow too tall for any but very large rock gardens. However, the following forms keep within a manageable scale.
C. japonica 'Compressa', h. 1m (40in), is a dense rounded plant with juvenile foliage that takes on a fine bronze colouring in winter.

JUNIPERUS
Many of the junipers, although low growing and mat forming, are too vigorous and spreading except for large rock gardens and banks. The following, however, are suitable for a small scale garden.
J. communis 'Compressa', h. 1m (40in), is an outstanding dwarf conifer making a miniature column of dense blue-green foliage. A group of three gives a strong vertical accent.
J. squamata 'Blue Star', h. 1m (40in), will take many years to reach its mature size. It is a dumpy plant with silver-blue foliage that is particularly brilliant in summer.

PICEA The spruces are generally large forest trees but among cultivated forms there are many that are slow growing and dwarf and suitable for a rock garden.

P. abies 'Little Gem', h. 75cm (30in), forms a dense hummock with miniature leaves that are bright green in summer.

P. mariana 'Nana', h. 30cm (12in), is useful in the small rock garden or even a sink garden. It makes a dense clump of soft grey-blue leaves.

P. pungens 'Globosa', h. 1.5m (60in), is certainly worth a place in the larger rock garden. The rigid branches carry sharp needles of a striking silver blue.

PINUS Dwarf pines tend to be rather expensive as they are all grafted stock and many of the cultivated forms, although slow growing, are likely to become too large. However, they are certainly worth planting in the large rock garden, their widely varying textures and forms giving the imaginative gardener plenty of scope.

P. sylvestris 'Beuvronensis', h. 1.5m (60in), is a handsome dwarf form of the Scots pine with blue-green needles. As a

A sink garden with rock garden plants and a dwarf conifer — *Salix boydii.*

young plant it is generally densely branched but it may become more open with age.

THUJA
It is not surprising that a genus that has given rise to so many excellent ornamental trees should also have produced dwarf forms that are beautiful as well as being easy to grow.
T. occidentalis 'Caespitosa', h. 25cm (10in), makes a rounded miniature bush with drooping green foliage.
T. o. 'Hetz Midget' is a similar plant but has golden foliage.
T. orientalis 'Aurea Nana', h. 1.5m (60in), is a strong yellow colour, particularly early in the summer. The vertical sprays are densely packed in a rounded bush.

TSUGA
The dwarf forms of the hemlocks are likely to become as popular in Europe as they are in the United States but the range currently available is still limited.
T. canadensis 'Bennett' and *T. c.* 'Jeddeloh', h. 1m (40in), are two forms with graceful drooping habit and mid-green foliage that is deliciously fresh when new.

FERNS AND GRASSES

Ferns and grasses are easily overlooked as subjects for the rock garden. These categories, however, include many beautiful plants of dwarf habit that do well in rock garden conditions, softening the edge of stone and providing a foil for more showy plants.

Most ferns need protection from full sun so it is possible to make a virtue of what are often considered difficult shady corners. The smaller ferns are particularly effective planted on a north-facing dry stone wall or among the blocks of a raised peat bed. Ideally, ferns should be planted in these positions during construction, the rhizomes or rootstocks being bedded in between rocks or peat blocks and well covered with a mixture of peat and loam. Most ferns are readily propagated by division and, for the patient gardener, there is the interesting possibility of raising plants from spores.

Many ferns show an astonishing capacity to produce spores with crested and frilled fronds. In the past these forms have been much sought after and there is currently renewed interest in them. They are not listed below but can be found in the catalogues of specialist nurseries.

ADIANTUM   Although many of the maidenhair ferns are rather tender plants there are several hardy enough for planting outdoors.
A. pedatum, h. 50cm (20in), a deciduous North American species, sends up fronds with a distinctive angular arrangement from creeping rhizomes. It is, perhaps, too large for the small rock garden but it is so beautiful it is worth stretching a point. A dwarfer subspecies, *A. p. aleuticum*, h. 15cm (6in), is of a more manageable size but is not easy to obtain.
A. venustum, h. 23cm (9in), is a mat-forming deciduous species that is especially attractive planted in a dry wall. The dead fronds take on warm copper tones in winter.

ASPLENIUM   The spleenworts, a huge genus that is represented in most parts of the world, include a number of hardy dwarf species well adapted to living in drystone walls. Most are more or less evergreen.
A. adiantum-nigrum, h. 10cm (4in), is a leathery tufted fern found in many parts of the world and easy in cultivation.
A. trichomanes, h. 10cm (4in), is a lime-loving species with wiry stems and neat rounded leaflets. Its refinement has earned it the common name maidenhair spleenwort.

Adiantum pedatum

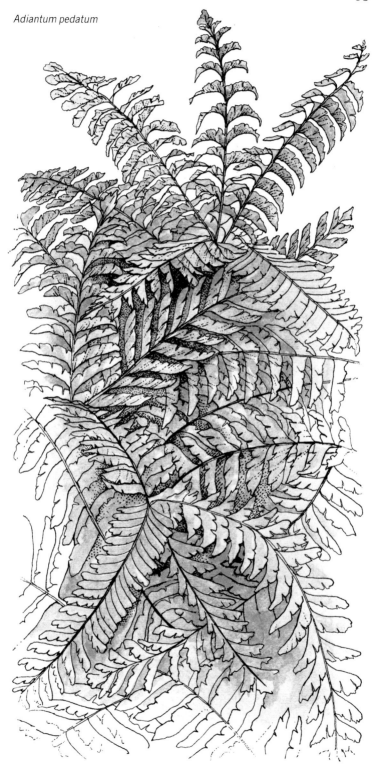

The ornamental value of perennial grasses, still too often thought of simply as weeds, can be exploited to good effect in the rock garden by strategic planting. Hummocky and spiky growth give interesting shapes and textures while blue-grey and golden foliage can provide a useful background to other plants. The flowerheads of most species are an added attraction but it is probably worth trimming heads before seeds ripen. Grasses do best in free draining sunny positions.

FESTUCA This widely distributed genus contains several fairly dwarf species.

F. alpina, h. 10cm (4in), makes a dense tuft of fine bright green leaves. The flowers, borne in late summer, are green tinged with violet.

F. ovina 'Glauca', h. 23cm (9in), forms a blue-grey bristling clump and has purple flowers in mid-summer. It is an effective plant in paving.

HAKONECHLOA One dwarf species of this genus, *H. macra-aurea*, h. 15cm (6in), is a particularly handsome golden-leaved grass.

Festuca ovina 'Glauca'

INDEX

*Numbers in italics
refer to illustrations*

96